"Vittoria, Look at Me,"

he said thickly. "Open your eyes and look at me."

A tremor of such fierce longing moved through Torey that she felt weak. She reached up and held him tightly, feeling power in the muscles across his back. He moved slowly against her and his fingers trailed lightly across her skin.

His mouth moved boldly on her, stirring a wild sea of desire. Each new kiss was a tiny wave eroding her resistance.

"Don't," she pleaded weakly, as fearful that he would listen and stop as that he wouldn't.

ANN HURLEY
sprang from a family chock-full of lawyers, teachers, and scientists, and married most happily into a family equally rich in artists, sculptors, architects, and musicians. After a long stint teaching literature and creative writing, Ann realized that, most of all, she wanted to write. Now, in between riding herd on her young daughter and the family's mammoth one-eyed black dog, Ann is writing for Silhouette.

Dear Reader:

Silhouette has always tried to give you exactly what you want. When you asked for increased realism, deeper characterization and greater length, we brought you Silhouette Special Editions. When you asked for increased sensuality, we brought you Silhouette Desire. Now you ask for books with the length and depth of Special Editions, the sensuality of Desire, but with something else besides, something that no one else offers. Now we bring you SILHOUETTE INTIMATE MOMENTS, true romance novels, longer than the usual, with all the depth that length requires. More sensuous than the usual, with characters whose maturity matches that sensuality. Books with the ingredient no one else has tapped: excitement.

There is an electricity between two people in love that makes everything they do magic, larger than life—and this is what we bring you in SILHOUETTE INTIMATE MOMENTS. Look for them wherever you buy books.

These books are for the woman who wants more than she has ever had before. These books are for you. As always, we look forward to your comments and suggestions. You can write to me at the address below:

Karen Solem
Editor-in-Chief
Silhouette Books
P.O. Box 769
New York, N.Y. 10019

ANN HURLEY
Touch of Greatness

Silhouette Special Edition
Published by Silhouette Books New York
America's Publisher of Contemporary Romance

SILHOUETTE BOOKS, a Simon & Schuster Division of
GULF & WESTERN CORPORATION
1230 Avenue of the Americas, New York, N.Y. 10020

Copyright © 1983 by Ann Hurley

Distributed by Pocket Books

ISBN: 0-671-53598-6

First Silhouette Books printing June, 1983

10 9 8 7 6 5 4 3 2 1

All of the characters in this book are fictitious. Any resem-
blance to actual persons, living or dead, is purely coincidental.

Map by Ray Lundgren

SILHOUETTE, SILHOUETTE SPECIAL EDITION and
colophon are registered trademarks of Simon & Schuster.

America's Publisher of Contemporary Romance

Printed in the U.S.A.

To Robert and Bianca

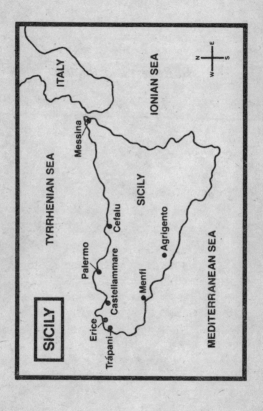

Chapter One

The Palermo airport was a chaos of noise and people. It was not modern or efficient; Torey had to paw through rope-tied parcels and cardboard suitcases until she found her own two bags. Long strands of her red-brown hair slipped out of the careful chignon Paola had arranged for her, and she pushed them back impatiently. There would be no one to meet her, and failing to grab a porter's arm, she smoothed down the wrinkles in the tan linen skirt and dragged her suitcases outside the stifling terminal.

"Ah, the lovely Mrs. Gardner," said a cheerful voice at her elbow. "May I offer you a ride to your hotel?"

It was the plump and pleasant businessman who had been her seatmate on the short flight from

Rome. He had been eager for conversation and, having heard her command of Italian, had tried very hard to engage her. There had been the usual introduction with a flourish of his business card. In the next twenty minutes he had extracted, with persistent and typical charm, all the pertinent information about her. Torey's attempts to be vague and aloof had failed miserably; there was no defense against the quick Italian mind that took monosyllabic answers and pieced together biographies. It used to amaze her when Paola did it, but she now saw that it was a common gift.

"You're very kind," she said, "but no, thanks. I'll catch a taxi to the apartment I've rented."

Recent experiences in Rome had taught her caution in dealing with Italian men. Everything had been friendly and casual on the plane when the little man had discovered she was American, not English, and had studied painting at the Academy in Rome. He had immediately recognized Paola Vizzini's name as a prominent fabric designer and had seemed duly impressed. He had complimented her on the silver ring of olive leaves she wore, the ring Jon had designed when they were married.

Foolishly, Torey had yielded to the warmth of his interested, sympathetic eyes and to the peculiar freedom of talking to a complete stranger, someone she would never see again. When he learned she had been widowed almost two years ago, her casual companion had instantly offered her a glass of wine, a moist and lingering pat on the hand and a growing predatory look. Caution! She must not forget.

A spring breeze swirled newspapers and candy

wrappers aloft in eccentric circles of dust. Waving her arm proved totally ineffectual, so Torey got a taxi by the simple, if foolish, method of stepping off the curb, forcing one to pull to a shrieking halt.

"Which hotel, lady?" the cab driver croaked at her. For a minute, Torey could not understand one word of the guttural Sicilian dialect. The man looked Arabic and sounded as if he were grating cheese deep in his throat. "Which hotel?"

Haltingly she gave the address on via Emma, and the man shook his head in a frenzy of disbelief. When she repeated herself, he slapped his flat cap against the steering wheel in frustration.

"That is not a hotel, dear lady. All tourists want the hotel district."

Italian was supposed to be light and fluid, not this hoarse, twisted mixture of sounds. Torey put some real authority in her voice and insisted on the address.

The man shrugged in resignation, and the cab negotiated a sharp U-turn, throwing her into the corner with bruising force, then shot off for the city thirty kilometers away. The driver ground the gears going top speed and constantly peered intently at her in the rearview mirror. Worst of all, he frequently turned around to look and talk over his shoulder.

This could be considered another bad omen, she thought fleetingly. The first was seeing monte Pellegrino, Palermo's famous mountain landmark, from the air. It had only been a pale, humped limestone whale, not a beautiful sight. Torey had laughed at Paola's recital of a sixteenth-century proverb warning that Sicily was a place inhabited by devils and visited by madmen. This cab driver, unfortunately, seemed to be possessed by a demon. She finally begged the man to slow down and was treated to a barely comprehensible speech about the poor quality of petrol, how low in octane, and how only speed forestalled the total collapse of the machine. The entire diatribe was accompanied by wild gestures of both hands that made the cab careen all over the road, so Torey abandoned herself to fate and said nothing more.

Roberto and Paola had tried so hard to dissuade her from leaving them and Rome. The last three days had been filled with constant coaxing, cajoling and pleading with her to stay. The Vizzinis were firmly convinced that a few more weeks could somehow accomplish what the past six months with them had failed to do. Paola wanted her to work at some fabric design. If Torey wasn't painting anymore, she must—the argument went—try something else artistic.

"What is there in life but love and work?" Paola had insisted in her passionate, winning way.

"Food," Roberto added without looking up from his legal brief.

How beautiful and good they were. Torey had turned at the foot of the plane's stairs that morning and waved at them—the perfect Roman couple: elegant, rich and civilized—with tears in her eyes. Roberto's practice was well established now; he dressed, ate, drank and talked the part of a young, successful lawyer to perfection. Paola's fabric business had flourished in the past two years; she had all the love and work she could handle. A pang of jealousy shot through Torey just thinking about them.

No, she had made a good decision to leave. It was such a struggle to be civil and reasonable when they had so many good arguments against this trip, alone, to Sicily. She knew no one, it was a primitive place, and on and on. But long ago she and Jon had planned to paint in Sicily, and now she was determined to try it. All the long walks, talks, endless parties and dinners in Rome had helped her enormously, she realized, to rejoin life around her, but a painter had to paint. And, she confided to Paola, the parade of eligible lawyers and bankers Roberto insisted on inviting only bored or depressed her. It had simply been time for her to get on with living and she needed to go alone.

Fumbling in her purse for comb and lipstick, Torey drew out the list Paola had pressed in her hand at Da Vinci Airport. Peppina Barbera's address was at the top. Peppina had worked for Paola's family for years, and Torey vaguely remembered meeting the woman when she and Jon had studied in Rome. But also listed were the numbers of Roberto's law firm, Paola's office, the American consul, the hospital in Rome. Everyone but the chief of police, Torey had joked, saying she felt as though she were on a field trip to study cannibals, not paint dusty landscapes.

The streets of Palermo teemed with cars, buses, motorbikes and pedestrians. Her driver did not slow down the taxi or his energetic commentary on the blurred sights as they flew past. The cab stopped abruptly on a narrow street in front of a three-story building, plastered a pale pink. As she counted out lire from the thick wad of bills, a troupe of children ran for the door of the cab. Torey frantically transacted business with the driver and watched helplessly as two of the older children dragged away her suitcases.

"*Ciao*, Rita Hayworth!" The driver blew her a good-bye kiss, laughed, and pulled back into traffic without a second's hesitation.

The strange remark made her laugh aloud. Her luggage had vanished into the building, and her hair was wildly blowing about her face and down her back. She felt nothing like a movie star. Two thin dogs fought not ten feet from her over a small heap of garbage. Her laughter might have turned to tears, but she felt herself lifted almost off her feet by a pair of wiry, skinny arms and locked in a mad embrace. Torey drew back quickly and found the assailant was a small older woman with a finely arched nose and deep, sunken eyes.

"Signora Barbera?" Torey found herself mesmerized by the blackness of the woman's eyes, astounded at the strength of such a little woman.

"Of course, but it must be Peppina to you, Victoria. I got Paola's call from Rome to expect you. My son, Gian-Carlo, and his friend took your bags upstairs to your rooms. My, you look tired but actually prettier than I remembered! Come in my place and we'll have some lemonade. You can sit and relax a few minutes, no?"

The Sicilians, Torey had been warned seriously, were violent, proud and reserved. So far she had met no one who fit that description.

In minutes Torey was installed in an ancient

sprung chair with a cold drink in one hand and balancing a plate of *biscotti*, the inevitable small cookies, on the other. One of the smaller children had pulled off her sandals and was admiring them. They all sat in the crowded living room opening directly on the street, and people seemed to be constantly coming or going, sticking their heads through the open window to exchange a few words and to openly gape at her.

"When Paola wrote me you were coming, I tried and tried to recall your face," said Peppina, brushing children away from her like cookie crumbs. "But it was so long ago. How old are you now?"

There it was again, the strange, direct inquiry, but from this bird of a woman, Torey couldn't take offense. "Twenty-seven."

"Such a pity you didn't have any children. When Gino died, I had my little ones for comfort," Peppina went on, aiming a slap at one of her comforts as he took another cookie meant for the guest. "Paola told me about the car accident and I was very sad for you. A great tragedy—such a talented young man!"

"How many children *do* you have?" Torey had given up counting all the different faces wandering through.

Peppina threw back her head and laughed. "These aren't all mine, just some of them. The two boys there, Gian-Carlo and Beppo; and my girl, Elizabetta, is hiding in the corner. My oldest son, Aldo, is away working."

There was no way to guess which two boys in the room Peppina meant, but the girl was pressed shyly against the far wall. Elizabetta looked about fourteen, pale and budding late for an Italian adolescent. Her face was an almost luminous oval surrounded by a cloud of light brown hair. She had not taken her eyes off Torey for a minute and she had not said one word.

"Perhaps," suggested Peppina, "you want to go up and look over your rooms? You just tell me if something isn't right and I'll have it fixed."

"Thank you," Torey sighed gratefully. "I would like to wash up and get settled. Maybe later this afternoon I'll go get a few things to eat." She was relieved by the suggestion. Her eyes burned with travel and dust; the small of her back sent out small electric shocks of protest.

"Betta," bellowed her landlady in a voice larger than she was, "take Mrs. Gardner upstairs."

The girl led the way on the winding stairs to the third floor, where the door stood partly open and Torey's suitcases had been neatly deposited. The apartment had three rooms. It was sparsely furnished but very clean.

The largest room was very spacious, perfect for painting, and held only an old gray couch with several hand-crocheted pillows arranged on it, a chair that matched the one in Peppina's house, and a small table and lamp. The wall over the street had large French doors leading to a stamp-sized balcony, so there would be plenty of light. Torey was instantly satisfied, but she dutifully followed Betta on the inspection.

The kitchen was minimally equipped, but the cupboards were freshly painted and water ran from the sink faucets. A battered wooden dining table was decorated with a potted scarlet geranium, an old corned beef tin planted with fresh mint and another plate of Peppina's *biscotti*. The attempts to make the place homey genuinely touched Torey.

Wordless, Betta waited nearby as Torey walked through the last room. The bedroom was completely filled by just a bed and an ancient armoire for clothes. The prize feature of the apartment was clearly the bathroom, private and therefore a rare treasure. It was, in fact, a remodeled closet and completely covered in sea-green tile. Torey had the distinct sensation of being underwater when she walked into it. It contained all the necessary equipment, however, and she was well aware of the value of a private bath in old Italian buildings.

A plaintive voice interrupted her thoughts. "Signora? Is it all right? I must tell Mamma."

"Call me Torey, please," she insisted quietly, admiring the girl's pose in the doorway and afraid of spooking her. "It's a fine place, and thank Peppina for the plants, the cookies and her kindness. This will be a wonderful studio to work in."

Elizabetta only dropped her head shyly in answer. She lingered at the door as if glued in fascination. Over her shoulder she whispered, "Are you a movie star?" and fled, clattering down the stairs before she could possibly get an answer.

I had to come to Palermo to be discovered, Torey thought. Rita Hayworth? Movie Star? It felt so good to laugh again; the tension of the whole morning eased perceptibly. Torey unpacked and hung up her clothes, still chuckling. It was a shockingly poor wardrobe to Paola's way of thinking. Roberto had complained at the airport that Paola needed two suitcases just for shoes when they vacationed.

The kitchen cupboards were fine for storing sketchbooks, blocks of paper and paints. The sink in Neptune's Palace, as she promptly dubbed the bathroom, squealed thinly and finally spit out a small trickle of ice-cold water, which she splashed on her face and wrists. A real bath, with the ancient plumbing to wrestle with, would be too much of a battle, and her last bit of energy had evaporated. Torey lay down on the worn chenille cover of the bed in her bra and slip.

The apartment reminded her vividly of the very first one she and Jon had lived in five years ago, newly married. She had felt safe there and perhaps that boded well for this place. A syrup of warm, golden light poured in through the curtains and cast lace shadows along the floor. As her body relaxed, she knew she would sleep and enjoyed the sweet languor overtaking her. She had suffered a solid year of terrible insomnia, and even now she dreaded the occasional frightening dreams that still plagued her. Dreams were to be avoided at all costs.

Waking a few hours later, Torey felt startled, like a child in a strange bed. It took a quick survey of the room to reassure her. She decided that a warm bath and clean clothes, followed by a brisk walk to pick up a few staples, would energize her. She stripped off her underwear and threw on the figured silk kimono, one of Paola's sinfully expensive gifts. She pulled her hair loose from the remains of the chignon and shook it free, ruffling the great, soft mass of it into a mane. With one hand raking through tangled hair and the other clutching the robe closed, she headed for the bathroom and heard a noise.

A thump followed the metallic clank. A muffled swear word in a distinctly masculine voice made her jump violently. Torey stepped into the doorway and saw the back of a man crouched awkwardly between the sink and the tub. A sound combining a sob and a moan escaped from her throat involuntarily. She peered, owl-eyed, and gripped harder at the front of the robe and the hairbrush she hadn't been conscious of clutching.

The workman finally recognized her presence by half turning, still squatted.

"I really think," he said in a rich baritone voice, "that this wrench will be sufficient for the job." He smiled broadly at the hairbrush she was pointing in his direction.

There were tools, wrenches and hammers of formidable size, arranged neatly to his left. The man stood up slowly in the cramped space and stared openly back at her, every bit as intent as she was. The small room made him look enormous, but he was easily six feet tall, lean and well muscled. His forearms were a darker tan where the light blue sleeves of his shirt were rolled back. His tight, well-worn jeans were spotted with water and flecks of rust. When Torey simply continued to stand there, he shrugged his broad shoulders and ran one hand through his black wavy hair in a common gesture of resignation. Then he turned and resumed work as if she did not exist.

"Who are you?" demanded a furious Torey, relieved she had finally found her voice. Fear had widened her gray-green eyes and speeded up her breathing. Anger at this intrusion sent a rush of blood to her cheeks, flushed pink under the golden skin, and spilled heat and color down her neck into the loose neckline. "What do you think you're doing here?"

The man didn't bother to turn back to reply. His hands, with powerful wrists and prominent veins, kept working on the protesting pipe joints.

"It should be obvious enough. I am trying to correct some of the worst plumbing in Palermo. Peppina insists everything must be perfect for such an important guest. You do want all the comforts of a fine hotel, eh?"

"Mr.—Mr. Plumber, I want you out," she stammered. "The water is fine, the pipes are adequate. I don't want you banging on the plumbing and leaving heaps of rust and what-all around. I want a bath and I want it now."

He looked up at her and raised one eyebrow. It was neatly split in two by a wide, white scar and made the mocking light in his blue eyes more emphatic. Torey pulled the robe closer at that look. The motion only accentuated, not minimized, the swell of her breasts and the curve of her waist.

"I have heard how fussy Americans are and how they demand their comforts," he said with a full grin. "There is coffee in the kitchen; I brought some with me. Why don't you just go have a cup—after you put on some clothes—and wait nicely until I finish here?"

The appraising look, the total arrogance of the

man, fueled the fire in her, but Torey tried to speak in an even, controlled tone. She was not going to let her temper get out of control.

"I have been traveling all morning," she began reasonably, "and I have a great many things to do. I don't want any interruptions. I would be very grateful if you simply left. I'll even pay you for your time so far. I'll tell Peppina myself that I didn't need your services so you won't have any problems with her."

"Ah-ha," he said, reaching for the pipe compound. "Rich tourists can always buy what they need or pay off the annoying peasants." Muscles in his back rippled against the cheap fabric of the shirt as he continued to work.

"You insufferable . . ." Torey took a step forward and unleashed the worst invective she knew, using all the choice phrases gleaned from the streets of Rome. She was trembling with indignation.

The man rose to face the verbal attack, and after a few minutes of fierce storm she sputtered to a calmer state. Torey noticed she had been threatening him with the hairbrush as if it were a sword and dropped her hand to her side in total embarrassment. She took a few deep breaths, suddenly and acutely aware of his physical nearness and the faint smell of fresh sweat and shaving lotion.

His eyes held only the coolest amusement at her performance. His finely chiseled mouth was drawn slightly back, hinting at another smile and suppressed laughter. Finally he did smile, revealing a magnificent and disarming grin.

"I certainly did not intend to frighten you, Mrs. Gardner," he said in a soothing way, "but I assume,

from your silly outburst, I did. The door was unlocked, the apartment seemed empty, and so I went
to work. Now I think we are even; I scared you and
you have roundly cursed me. With or without your
permission, I will finish the work here."

There was absolutely nothing she could do. Her
reaction was all out of proportion, and if she was still
irritated, Torey also felt quite sheepish. He was
aggravating and outspoken, but the water system
was badly in need of repair.

"All right," she conceded, "but please do it as
quicky as possible."

"It took almost a hundred years for this piping to
deteriorate, but I understand that foreigners have no
sympathy with the problems of the old. I give you
my word I will work as fast as I can."

Dammit, he had gotten in the last word! Torey
whipped around and marched almost stiff-legged
with fury into the bedroom. Grabbing brown slacks
and a tan sweater, she dressed and brushed her hair
out. The furious strokes made static electricity crack-
le, but the act relieved her of some of the prickly
feelings within her. A thermos was standing on the
kitchen table and she poured some steaming coffee
into the thermos top.

The door was standing wide open, and although
she had not locked it—an obvious mistake—she
couldn't recall leaving it ajar. Torey slammed it
closed, delighted to find another harmless outlet for
her tension.

His voice boomed out of the bathroom, "Leave
that door open, Mrs. Gardner. You're in Sicily
now."

Puzzling over the cryptic remark, she finished her coffee and poured another cup. As long as she was forced to wait, she took out a few sheets of paper and worked on some thumbnail sketches. It was difficult to concentrate with a background of thuds and metallic clanks, but the last sketch of Betta's pose in the doorway pleased her. She propped it up and studied it critically.

"Very nice line," he said from behind her. "You got Betta's sweetness nicely."

His walk was loose and athletic and he sat down next to her, totally at home. It seemed unlikely that those clear, startling blue eyes missed much of anything, but he gave her no sign that he recognized the wave of uneasiness that swept her. Torey couldn't help appreciate the grace of his slim-hipped stride and the erect but relaxed posture of the man. What a model he'd make, she thought.

He picked up the cup at her elbow and sipped the coffee she'd poured for herself.

"Sugar, signor . . . ?" She let her sarcastic tone trail off in a clear question.

"Scarpi," he said. "My name is Andrea Scarpi, and I don't take sugar, thanks."

"You could use some, Mr. Scarpi," Torey replied pointedly. She found herself wanting to needle him. It wasn't merely the calculating look he gave her; she was used to the head-to-toe appraisal of Italian men. They felt they were required to do that. No, there was something else about him that elicited this reaction.

"I have been told before my manners are a bit sharp, Vittoria Gardner."

"In English, the name is Victoria," she insisted. Actually, she had always hated her name, with its regal, cold implications, but she wanted to correct this man and put him firmly in his place. Don't be such a jerk, she quickly chided herself. If she was pleasant, perhaps he'd sit for her. "Mr. Scarpi, let's start again. I apologize for the . . . difficulty we had. I must admit I was surprised and frightened and I reacted badly."

"You are a surprise to me too," he said. "When Peppina went on and on at great length about her prospective guest, I had pictured one of those older American ladies with pale blue hair in lots of tight little curls, glasses on a chain and sensible walking shoes. I'm sure you know what I mean—the little widow who comes to Sicily to play at painting our cute carts and donkeys. . . ."

She found herself speechless again. Had it really been necessary to inform every tenant and workman of her visit, her credentials, her whole life story? She refused to let him banter with her like this.

"I'm not represented in the Uffizi Gallery or the Vatican collection, but I have shown in Chicago and Rome at the Academy and a few small galleries." As she spoke, she watched his face, wondering how it would be possible to capture the sweep of his high cheekbones and the classic line of his jaw. A three-quarter view? "You don't seem to like artists, or is it just tourists you dislike?"

"Art is a fine thing, but it is hard to eat a painting. As for the tourists, I have found very little to like about any of them. A lady artist with such a sharp tongue is an entirely new experience for me."

"I do apologize," repeated Torey, forcing sincerity into her voice. "I tend to get angry when I am fearful."

He laughed heartily. "Then why would a woman, looking like she expected to be eaten alive, come here to the ancient land of wolves? I'm sure your important Roman friends told you all about the barbarians on this island and how we relish a tender traveler for breakfast."

"I came here to work and find something different than Rome offered. It's really very simple."

He picked up the soft lead sketching pencil and ran his fingers up and down it. He had good, well-modeled hands with long, straight fingers. Unthinking, Torey reached for the pencil, afraid he would break it. The look he flashed her actually chilled her; there was a clear element of warning in it. She drew away from him abruptly.

"Nothing in life is simple, Mrs. Gardner, especially in Sicily," he said in his deep, cultured voice. His Italian was not tinged with the coarseness of the local dialect. "Your trip here could teach you a lot if you are a good pupil."

He rose from the chair in one easy and fluid motion, as if a spring had uncoiled, and with a curt nod to her, went to the door.

"I've finished now, and I tried not to leave you too much of a mess. I could send Betta up to clean, if you like."

"That won't be necessary, Mr. Scarpi. I'm capable of managing myself," Torey said, relieved at his imminent departure. She bent her head over another sheet of paper and busied herself until he had closed the door firmly behind him. The sound of his voice in the stairwell calling to Peppina drifted back to her.

It was a bizarre encounter when she thought about it, and yet it seemed to fit perfectly into the whole disquieting day. A plumber who looked like a statue by Phidias and spoke in the clever, sarcastic manner of a well-bred Roman didn't fit into the Sicilian mold. He was the rudest man she had encountered in a long time—but, she admitted ruefully, the most attractive one. Her well-trained eye had enjoyed his physique and features, more classically Greek than Roman.

Warm water gushed freely into the tub; the man's work had really been of some use. Luxuriating in a bath had the desired effect on her. Torey, relaxed and comfortable, began to organize her thoughts, trying to decide what she wanted to accomplish while here on the island. Supposedly, there were few places in the world with as many different vistas, colors and textures that also had the virtue of not having been done to death by artists. Jon had once told her that the light alone in Sicily was supposed to be totally strange, unlike anywhere else in the world.

Totally strange. Her first hours here were surely that and more. This might be a few weeks of surprises after all. She recalled the sketch of Betta and it seemed a good promise of things to come. Every time Torey had picked up a brush in the last few months, she had had to throw it down in disgust. It had been too long since she had felt enthusiasm or the stirrings of new ideas.

The armoire door had a mirrored front, and now,

as she passed it, her reflection flashed in a corona of sunlight. Trailing drops of water and leaving dark footprints, Torey paused to step closer and watch herself, always objective. In this last year her body had gotten much thinner. Jon had liked her plump and rounded, kidding her about "baby fat" and claiming he didn't like protruding bones on his favorite model. Her face was slightly drawn but tanned, looking good against the deep, rich color of her hair. Her eyes had an almost oriental shape, despite the peculiar coloring. A real beauty wouldn't have had her thin, straight nose and the full, too-generous mouth, but it pleased her when her husband had pronounced her "handsome."

There was very little vanity to Torey and she knew the reason. A gawky, painful adolescence as a tall and chubby girl with braces and wildly waving hair had colored her view of herself for all time. She could never shake that earlier vision of herself completely. She stared critically at her body—the full, dark-crowned breasts, the slender waist and the flaring of hips—and began to dress hurriedly. A thought, unbidden and completely crazy, had occurred to her, seeing herself in the mirror.

What if she had walked in on that Scarpi man naked? He might not have been so arrogant, so unfailingly quick with a smart remark. It would have been enjoyable to shake up such an obstinate man and crack the imperturbable ice of his manner. It was a crazy thought. She wasn't an exhibitionist, even if she wasn't particularly modest, and she didn't understand the thought at all. His overconfident manner had really nettled her, she decided.

She brushed her hair until it fell into a thick, slightly curling mass and shone red-gold where the afternoon sun touched it. She grabbed her purse and the sketch, intending to ask Betta to pose formally for her. Before she left, Torey double-checked the lock on the door. She didn't care to be caught so off-balance again.

Chapter Two

"Sit down and have a roll with Betta," insisted Peppina, scrubbing the oilcloth on her kitchen table. "I'll be ready to go marketing in a minute. Are the rooms what you wanted? Did you find the small store around the corner? Betta, don't stare at Mrs. Gardner as if you were simpleminded, God forbid!"

"To all the questions, yes," said Torey. "It's just what I wanted. No, no, Betta, don't leave."

The girl promptly sat down and watched from under long, thick eyelashes. She pulled self-consciously at a tight, faded green sweater and gathered more details about the guest. Torey insisted Betta share a small bread roll thickly spread with peach jam and watched as the girl dumped two heaping spoons of sugar into her own coffee. When

Torey pretended to be busy eating, Betta hastily slipped in another spoonful.

"Are you really very rich, Mrs. Gardner?" Betta blurted out through a hefty bite of roll.

"Torey, please. No, I'm not, and I'm not a movie star, either! Whatever gave you the idea I'm rich or famous?" Torey thought of the rapidly dwindling money she had arrived in Rome with and the still untouched insurance money in Chicago.

"You have three whole rooms for just one person, a bath for yourself and a bed that will hold four of us." The girl's eyes were a rich velvet brown flecked with the tiniest sequins of gold and totally innocent.

"Now, Betta, be still," threatened her mother, embarrassed.

"I'm a painter, as you know," explained Torey. "I need room to work in as well as live in. Don't scold her, Peppina, it's all right. I'm from Chicago, Betta. Do you know anything about Chicago?"

There was a short pause and then an affirmative shake of the head. *"Si,* I know Elliot Ness and 'The Untouchables' on the television."

Torey could barely stifle her laughter. "Well, it's not exactly like that anymore, believe me. But I'll bet people come to Sicily and ask to see the Mafia."

The bread roll had completely vanished, and Betta seemed visibly easier in her presence.

"Did you come all the way to Palermo to paint us? Do you want to paint my picture?"

"That little drawing I showed you yesterday was only a beginning. If you'll pose for me, I'll do more sketches and finally a painting of you. That is, if you like. . . ." Torey added, but there was no mistaking the excited, animated look crossing Betta's face.

"Mamma, think of it! A real painting of me by a real artist."

Torey reached across the table and smoothed back the girl's ragged bangs.

"I wouldn't bother you," promised Betta. "I won't be any problem. Mamma said we mustn't bother you."

Torey glanced quickly at Peppina. What had been said to seemingly everyone in Palermo?

"Let's go, Torey," said Peppina in her throaty voice. "If we don't get there early, all the best stuff is gone."

Torey waited until they were well down the street, both armed with their net bags, on the way to the food market. Politely but firmly she asked the older woman exactly what information about her had been offered to the children and "other people."

Peppina stopped, drew herself up defensively and protested, "I am the soul of discretion, as Paola must have told you. I said only that you were a good friend of the Vizzinis, that you had suffered a great tragedy and you needed a vacation. Only that."

Knowing the Italian love of the dramatic, Torey suspected that was not all, but she felt it was useless to pursue the subject further. Peppina had stiffened her back and compressed her lips into a thin line in outrage at being suspected of gossiping. It would hardly do to alienate her landlady.

The flow of their conversation resumed and then was interrupted as they dodged the bicycles and motorbikes. Peppina had to stop frequently to trade certain choice bits of "news." Torey found herself the object of great curiosity; very few tourists strayed away from the luxurious hotel district and fewer spoke Italian with any fluency. She also accepted the good-natured kidding as Peppina's neighbors dropped in and out of dialect, making Torey struggle hard to follow a conversation.

Her eye took in the tumult of the streets around them, all din and dust and motion. Mentally she began to sketch a particularly striking face or a graceful gesture, filing away the aggressive stance of a postcard vendor who stood shrieking tonelessly on the corner. Peppina led her through a maze of winding alleys lined with makeshift stands and laundry flapping overhead like flags. Everything was being hawked, from garishly painted miniature Sicilian horses and carts to lottery tickets, sunglasses and woven raffia hats. As they approached the food stands, the sounds became wilder and the smells, stronger. Peppina pushed aside a mob of children and Torey stopped, amazed at the kaleidoscopic view before her.

A thousand large umbrellas of white and cream and stained beige hovered like a flock of sea gulls over a vast sea of food. In the intense glare of the sun, mounds of small, hard tomatoes glowed scarlet next to elaborately built temples of gleaming black eggplants. There were sausages and cheeses hung in long garlands, exotic and aromatic flowers. Small Mount Etnas had been constructed of green and purple olives and then, ridiculously but delightfully, crowned with fresh blooming rosemary. Even the overpowering stench of fish could not put Torey off; the hundreds of strange varieties from the morning's catch were arranged in a mosaic of Byzantine splendor. And everywhere, people crawled among the crowded stalls, worshipping the joy of food.

Peppina scrambled nimbly from one favored seller to the next, arguing at length, even nastily, about the price and quality of every squash and string of onions. She would hold out a melon and beg Torey to look at this miserable offering for six hundred lire. Torey would obligingly confer with her to the delight of the vendor. He would then plead for the support of his ten children and swear every vegetable and fruit he sold would nourish all of them. The game was an essential part of the process; Torey had enjoyed playing it with Paola in much fancier stores in Rome.

"Let me buy a chicken," insisted Torey. "I can get two for one with some Roman charm."

Peppina agreed. "But only if you have dinner with us tonight."

The long string of poultry, plucked naked except for tail feathers, swayed gently on a wire over their heads. The argument took a full fifteen minutes and involved several bystanders as witnesses to the virtues of the skinny birds. After a satisfactory debate and sale, Torey presented Peppina with both birds, insisting she wanted to leave and start sketching while the scene was still fresh in her mind. The chickens moved awkwardly from side to side like bedraggled ballet dancers with tail-feather skirts.

The sun had risen higher, striking the back of Torey's neck with a strength that gave her chills. Everyone began to huddle in the shadows of bergamots, lemons and oranges for protection. The fury of the harsh voices was joined by the church bells, tolling madly from all parts of the city. There was a small cafe on the corner of the next alley and Torey fled into the cool dark sanctuary it offered, feeling her senses had been bruised by the incredible sights and sounds of the market.

A cool drink helped calm her, but she decided not to tackle the Street of Shoes Paola had described to her. She was not sure her brain could take more stimulation. Torey gathered up her purchases as two women, obviously tourists, came into the dim room.

They pushed past her and went directly to the bar, where one of them ordered Cokes in bad Italian. The other girl, pretty and with a striking tan, kept up a steady chatter in English to her friend. Torey resisted the impulse to strike up a conversation. Sometimes she desperately missed the familiar sounds of English. The woman who spoke some Italian asked the barman where the Church of San Francesco was located, and Torey blanched.

All of Andrea Scarpi's nasty comments and disdain for tourists flooded over her and she felt acutely uncomfortable. The women wore skimpy T-shirts and shorts. She debated briefly with herself if she should suggest that they would be refused entrance to a church and that they were not dressed in the best possible taste.

"Forget it," the tanned one said loudly, "and let's

go back to the hotel and swim. Have you ever seen such a collection of stone faces? What a down place this is!"

Torey fled before she heard any more. She threaded her way back to via Emma, her head bursting with ideas for sketches. A knot of women dressed completely in black parted to let her by; she noticed several of them held one corner of their black shawls tightly in their teeth, almost a parody of the harem veil.

She was and had always been a landscape painter. Her work was tight, controlled and almost geometric in its application of light and pastel colors. Now she was thinking only in terms of the people and their faces. Instead of being fascinated by the play of the sun on the pink apartment building, Torey stood watching Peppina's boys throw coins at the base of the wall. They waved at her politely but would not interrupt their game to chat.

The older boy, Gian-Carlo, reminded Torey of a Renaissance angel with his short curly hair haloed about a dirt-streaked face. The little boy of nine, Beppo, had two scabby knees that brought back childhood memories in a rush. The "baby," as Peppina referred to him, was as pale and scrawny as one of the unfortunate chickens in the market. She wondered if they went to school; they seemed to always be around.

She hurried up the stairs with more energy than she had felt in months, compelled to get the bare outlines of all the images running through her brain down on paper before they faded. Above all else, she wanted to translate some of the wildness of color and movement to be sure she still could work after all these terrible, empty months.

Her hand raced across the clean, fine pressed surface of the paper recreating the scenes: the market; Peppina arguing with a vendor; the chickens dancing on their wire; a ragged child running through the streets; and the two girls in the cafe. The lines flowed and merged into loose and fluid images and she worked steadily, without hesitation or criticism. She was particularly pleased with another sketch of Betta drawn from memory. It was simple and yet captured the girl on the edge of womanhood, eager and frightened all at once. Torey put the Conté crayon down and looked at it for long minutes.

The idea of trying to recreate Andrea Scarpi's face intrigued her, but suddenly all her earlier spontaneity left. She decided she wouldn't push herself at first. In one day, she had accomplished more real, tangible work than in the last two years. It felt wonderful.

Across the city the horizon was a golden ocher laced with a band of impossible red-purple clouds. Torey washed up and changed her wrinkled clothes for the sleek emerald slacks and natural string knit sweater she'd bought in Rome. Her favorite silver and green enamel hoops were in the jewelry case, and she fished them out along with a large silver barrette. She surveyed the sketches again to reassure herself she really and truly had done a day's work and then went downstairs to help Peppina with the dinner.

The landlady clapped her hands together in praise

of the newest drawing of Betta. Torey had to suffer a rib-rattling hug and a sharp miss-nothing appraisal of herself.

"You are pleased with this one yourself, aren't you, Torey? Betta, come here and see this picture," shrilled Peppina.

"Betta is a fine model and it worked out very well," admitted Torey. "It feels so wonderful to work again. I can't tell you how good I feel."

"Will I be famous now?" chimed in Elizabetta, admiring herself.

"Only when and if I am," Torey assured her.

Peppina gave the girl a playful punch on the shoulder, saying, "You think too much about being famous or important. Believe me, it's much better to be happy and well fed."

"Rich and famous people are always happy and well fed," argued Betta with a child's certainty.

"Not the ones I know, you fresh thing," Peppina said. "Mrs. Gardner could make you immortal like Mona Lisa, and you'd still want more. Come and help with dinner before your head swells up and explodes."

"I want to help too," offered Torey.

Peppina protested that the kitchen was too small, too hot and too crowded, but she was openly pleased and gave in. Betta and Torey set up an assembly line to set the table. When Betta laid six plates and left to borrow a chair from the neighbors, Torey mentally counted and grew uncomfortable. She hated the thought of imposing if it was a family or special occasion. Aldo! It might be the older son.

"I must be very careful while I'm here," Torey said, sniffing rich and unfamiliar odors from the stove. "Either that or I'll have to buy two seats on the plane back to Rome to hold me."

Peppina stopped stirring and ran a calculating eye over her guest. "You could use a little more flesh. I suspect you have not been eating well, no matter what my foolish daughter thinks about rich foreigners."

"Not eating well, sleeping well or thinking straight," admitted Torey, "but that all, thank heavens, seems to be over now. I could devour everything in sight if I let myself."

"Good, *cara,* good," Peppina laughed. "This is a healthy sign, I think. Sorrow robs us of all our appetites, as we Sicilians say, but there is a time to let go."

Torey noted the use of the common Italian endearment. If she was "dear," it meant acceptance into Peppina's confidence. The thought pleased her inordinately and made her decide to speak more freely.

"Do the children go to school, Peppina? They all seem so bright and interested, but I notice they are usually home."

Peppina attacked the oranges she was slicing with a thinly disguised anger.

"The boys go to school, much good it will do them. Betta was so quiet and shy, I doubt they have noticed she is gone. School? For what? You have to learn about the way life is in Sicily to understand. There is no work to speak of here and great poverty. I'm not speaking about us, in particular. My Gino crossed Italy from one end to the other to find a week's work here and there."

Peppina crossed herself piously at the mention of her husband, and then mixed oil, lemon juice and black olives in with the oranges for a salad. She looked up at Torey in the doorway and shrugged.

"We were lucky," she continued, ladling food into dishes. "Gino died in Milan, all alone, without a word to his wife or four children. I thought it might be the end of us, that we'd starve or worse." She nodded toward Betta in the next room. "She might have gone north to go on the streets. But we had a touch of greatness in our lives. . . ."

Beppo dashed full speed into the room with a huge white cardboard box and an armful of flowers. Outside Torey could hear wild shrieks of delight.

"Speak of the devil and he will appear," said Peppina, taking the carnations and stuffing the baker's box into the refrigerator. She straightened up and saw the look on Torey's face. "Don't look so uncomfortable, *cara*. It's only Andrea, our dear friend. Whenever he comes to Palermo he has dinner with us."

The name was a common one, but Torey knew with instant and sinking surety that it was the plumber. She hoped it would not be a terrible evening.

"The plumber?" she said faintly. "I met him yesterday and I must tell you . . ."

Peppina was laughing so hard she had to wipe the corners of her eyes on her apron.

"Yes, the plumber Scarpi, the electrician Scarpi,

the painter and furniture mover Scarpi and the guardian angel of us all. He owns this building, Victoria."

"Well." Torey tried to smile. "He did seem a little strange for a plumber."

"I should hope so. No, *cara,* he is a structural engineer and builds bridges, dams, lots of big projects all over the island. He happens to own a few buildings as well and he always visits with us, bringing a something or two for the children. Did you two speak English? His English is very good, I'm sure."

"I screamed, I didn't speak," Torey said lamely. "I thought he had broken into the apartment and I carried on like a madwoman. I feel like a perfect idiot."

"No one is perfect though, Mrs. Gardner," he said. Andrea came into the kitchen with two bottles of wine in his right hand. His face was composed, but the blue eyes she remembered so well were dancing with undisguised mischief.

Peppina wiped her hands off, stood on tiptoe to kiss him on both cheeks and hugged him. She spoke in rapid dialect, exclaiming over his well-cut gray suit and tan. Andrea Scarpi looked directly at Torey over her head during the entire conversation.

"I just returned two days ago from Menfi, Mrs. Gardner," he said, explaining the tan, "and the sun is much stronger there."

"Yes," said Torey, trying hard to match this elegant and slim man with the plumber of yesterday. "I was just telling Peppina about something strong myself. Strong words that we had at our unfortunate meeting?"

He laughed and the corners of his eyes tilted upward. It was hard not to be impressed with his straight bearing and, most of all, the complete sense of ease he radiated. Torey had never met a person so comfortable and sure of himself.

"Actually," he said, "I don't recall swearing at all. I found our little talk interesting and the meeting fortunate. I hope now, however, as long as we are properly introduced and chaperoned"—Peppina dug her elbow into his ribs and cackled—"we can dispense with the formalities and be just Andrea and Victoria."

His very careful emphasis of her correct name was to twit her. It was obvious Andrea liked games.

"Just call me Torey," she said, and smiled broadly, determined to turn on the charm and show him she didn't rattle easily all the time.

"Everything is ready but the pasta," announced Peppina, urging them both toward the living room. "Betta will help me, and you two wait a few minutes."

"A few minutes can mean five minutes or an hour to an Italian," said Andrea, taking her arm. "You must know this by now, I'm sure. Beppo, please run out to the car and get me my cigars. They're on the seat."

It was ridiculous, but Torey jumped at his touch. As soon as Beppo left the room, she felt him focus his attention on her and she moved away from him deliberately. There was no playfulness in his eyes now and he walked purposefully to the mantel where the two sketches of Betta were displayed.

"You told the truth, Victoria. You are really an artist." His voice sounded almost annoyed, as if he refused to believe he might have misjudged her. "After seeing flocks of people come and go, you seem to have an open eye to the beauty of Sicily and her people."

"Why else would so many people come here, if not for the beauty?"

He smiled without humor, very slightly. "At least seven historical invasions have occurred here. They all were people who found reasons to conquer and drain this island. The tourist stampede is only the latest, as far as I'm concerned."

Torey found herself toying with her silver ring, turning it round and round in a nervous state. She wanted to avoid staring at his stark and handsome features. Keep it light, she thought, and easy. But it was difficult under the intensity of his gaze and obvious emotion.

"You don't look old, Andrea, and yet you manage to make it sound as if you'd lived through it all."

"I feel it deeply," he said. "Everyone who touched these shores took something away and left us poorer. Some took the riches from the earth and now they take pictures with their thirty-five-millimeter cameras, but Sicily is always plundered and left poorer. You might be different, or am I wrong?"

He offered her a drink, bringing out a bottle of Campari from the window cabinet.

"I don't care for it, thanks," Torey said quietly. "It's too bitter for my taste."

"Another hint?" he asked, pouring her a small glass of almond liqueur. "I am too bitter, too blunt for your taste?"

She chose to ignore the question, sipping the warm, sweet drink and savoring its flavor. "This is delicious."

"Don't try too hard to be amiable this evening, please." He sat next to her on the couch. "I think I prefer the lioness to a polite mouse. Do you find it difficult to talk to me, or would you just prefer to be alone?" His muscled leg in the tight, soft material brushed against hers.

She felt overwhelmed by him and by his closeness. In Rome, it had been a chore to sit and listen to the drone of dinner companions and try to pretend interest. Now she was fascinated and frightened by this stranger to an extent she couldn't pretend to understand.

"I don't prefer anything," she said shortly. "I don't like to be patronized, and if you detect a certain tension, I'm sorry."

This time his smile reached into his eyes and warmed them. "You say 'I'm sorry' a lot, it seems. What is it you are sorry about? I find you a very interesting and attractive woman, *bella*." His voice was deeper and more intimate, and his lips formed the word for beautiful as if it were a kiss.

She rejected the compliment. "I am sorry I find it impossible to have a pleasant, if meaningless, conversation with you. I am sorry you think it's all right to lecture or goad me into an argument." She longed to add that she was sorry he was so arrogant, irritating and well aware of how good-looking and magnetic a man he was.

Peppina poked her head into the room to announce dinner. A curtain of tension, almost palpable, hung across the room between them. She bustled around, seating Andrea at the head of the table and flanking him with Betta and Torey. Peppina would not sit down at all and hurried back and forth, bringing in dish after dish, pouring wine and muttering inaudibly to herself.

Andrea took off his suit coat and loosened his tie with the air of a bullfighter. Betta immediately launched into a long description of the fabric and ring Andrea had brought her from Menfi.

"Pretty things for pretty girls," he said, and kissed her thin hand in a courtly gesture.

The boys wanted to hear about the construction of Carboi Dam, so Andrea obliged with an animated discussion of the work while Gian-Carlo and Beppo ate as much and as quickly as they could. He was entirely different when he spoke to the children, Torey noted. He was patient and gentle without a trace of the cutting edge he used with her.

The food was marvelous and Torey was lavish with her praise. Peppina had transformed two lean chickens into a subtle sweet-and-sour dish, *pollo agrodolce*. The cook only smiled broadly at the compliments and insisted she eat more of the eggplant, tomato and caper mixture.

"This is simple peasant cooking, Torey, compared to the northern dishes you are used to."

"This is great!" Torey insisted. "I was expecting something entirely different."

"What?" Andrea demanded with a sidelong glance. "What did you expect?"

Before Torey could frame an answer, Peppina jumped in. "Sicilian men"—she shook a finger under his nose—"have more ego than brains. She wasn't offering an insult; she was never here and didn't know what to expect. It's an expression, you fool."

"Don't you start with me, old woman," Andrea said in a menacing tone, "or you'll ruin our image as savages." He grabbed the finger, bared his teeth as if he would bite it and then kissed Peppina's hand to make her laugh.

Torey sat frozen in high confusion. There was apparently no malice to any of these arguments. She decided if there were no mental institutions on the island it was because the inmates were running them.

"There is a quieter side to our nature," Andrea said, as if he'd read her mind. "A true pastoral element, and when Palermo gets too much for you, I'd like to show you the peaceful, gentle aspect."

Torey tore off a hunk of bread viciously. "Whyever would you think Palermo would be too much for me?" Her blood was racing and she felt drunk for some inexplicable reason. She hadn't touched her wine.

He answered her in a beautiful, barely inflected English. "I saw more in your sketches of Betta than her shyness and the imminent change in her. I think there was a quest for tranquil moments for yourself.

Palermo, unfortunately, is what Shakespeare said: 'All sound and fury, a tale told by . . .'"

"An idiot," she finished, and stared right back into his probing eyes. Here was a man so perceptive and intelligent that she found it hard to stay angry with him. There was a growing sense of admiration and, if she wanted to admit it, a strong physical attraction.

"Yes, I think Palermo could overwhelm you, *cara.*" He marveled at how stunning she was, color high on her cheeks and her eyes now very green with some hidden emotion. He had found her lovely yesterday, but he also sensed, intuitively, a deeper, troubled aspect. There were moments tonight when that shadow had appeared again, a dullness to life, but when Torey grew interested or angry, she was breathtaking. He speculated how she would look with a man, opened with passion, and then quickly suppressed the thought because it stirred him physically.

"This city even overwhelms me at times," he added. "I am relieved to leave it and yet glad when I come back."

Torey was aware of the looks from Peppina and Betta and asked him in Italian if he traveled a lot, and the dinner continued on a different, easier note. There were small jokes, a report on Aldo's progress learning the olive oil business near Agrigento, a discussion of Andrea's next project on the Jato Dam and a trip to London he was planning. Over coffee and dessert, they discussed art and argued only a little. Torey was amazed at his knowledge of current trends and relatively unknown artists.

She knew what was happening to her and felt completely powerless to stop it. Not long ago Torey had been brutally honest, telling Paola she had no interest, sexual or emotional, in any of the men the Vizzinis had been so eager to weave in and out of her life the last several months. Sometimes she had wished she could have a temporary, calculated affair to prove she was still a woman with real needs. It wasn't her style and it hadn't happened. But the man across the table this night was not boring, not a depressant. The feeling of warmth in her stomach was not wine; it became a brighter heat when she looked too long at his mouth or watched his hands cradle the cup.

"Will you take your boy with you to London?" asked Peppina.

"No," he said firmly, "he can't leave school for another long trip for a while. The good sisters won't even consider it."

Torey felt lost and safe in the same instant. You fool, she chided herself, of course he has a family and a wife and, if it's cold in winter, a mistress. It was stupid to imagine this man was unmarried. You can stop any fantasy right now.

"Does your family live here in Palermo, or do they travel with you?" Her voice had a hint of unsteadiness she despised.

Andrea's ear picked up the faint waver and held on to it in triumph. She wasn't indifferent to him or merely annoyed. The look on her face betrayed an interest, however slight, hidden behind innocent words.

"Benedetto has no mother and I have no wife,

45

Torey," he replied evenly. "I hope you didn't think me a man who flirts while playing the dutiful husband at home. I'm not flattered."

"I wasn't aware there was a flirtation going on," stammered Torey. It disconcerted her more to have been so transparent than to have made a mistake in her perception of him. "Be what you are or whatever you like."

"Good advice for everyone, I'm sure. You don't entirely follow your own dictum though, do you?"

"Where did you learn to be so infuriating?" she said, more in control. "Is there a school for bullies next to the College of Engineering?"

"Bravo," interjected Peppina. "Watch yourself, Scarpi. This American learns fast."

"She fights dirty, too," said Andrea. "When I say one thing, I'm a bully. Earlier, I was a pedant. What can I do to please the lovely Mrs. Gardner?"

He tried to look crestfallen but failed miserably and laughed instead. It was such an open, infectious laugh at himself that Torey joined in. Suddenly he reached across the table and took her hand, pulling it to his lips. His mouth brushed gently across the back of it, the touch of his breath warming it.

"And if I do this," he said in a whisper, his low, resonant voice running through her like a cool wind, "you will probably say I am a Romeo."

"I don't know what or who you are," Torey admitted, "or why you would concern yourself with pleasing 'Mrs. Gardner.'" She left her hand in his.

He turned it over, palm up, and stroked each finger, tapering and strong, wanting to choose exactly the right words to express his growing sense of her. "You are going to be here such a short time, and yet you made no reply when I asked you what you expected of this place. When someone is so obviously searching, I can't help wonder what you want, what you're hoping to find?"

"Contentment," Torey answered flatly. "I'm just not sure anything will ever content me again. Perhaps I was too complacent and self-satisfied for such a long time. Now . . ." Her eyes took on a silvery shine and their color grayed to a softer shade.

"Che spreco . . . what a waste," Andrea murmured. "There is such a sense of defeat and surrender in those words, Torey. It's not right for a woman, young and skilled. Contentment is a goal for the old, sitting quietly together and sharing memories. Don't grow old and find you have contented yourself with nothing!" He kissed the palm of her hand and closed her fingers tightly over, sealing the kiss inside.

In the absolute stillness of her room later, she looked at her hand carefully, as if it belonged to a total stranger. Torey undressed and lay down. The thin material of her nightgown felt confining and hot, so she slid it off, dropping it next to the bed. She knew she wanted to see him again and yet the possibility—the probability—was upsetting. Torey pressed her open hand to her burning cheek, feeling an immediate response like a chill through her body. It was as if she had transferred the touch of his mouth.

Chapter Three

*E*lizabetta had eagerly volunteered to be Torey's guide to the city. She took the job with grave seriousness, marking small blue circles on Palermo's map for points of general interest and red crosses where all the important churches were located.

"Byzantine style or Arab influence? Which do you like better, Torey?"

"I like your dress more than I can tell you, Betta. That's a wonderful color on you." She watched the girl straighten with pride and show off her pale peach cotton dress piped in rust.

"I made it myself and finished it last night especially to wear today," crowed Betta.

"I wish I could sew," Torey said honestly. "I never could follow a pattern or do more than stitch on a button. Once I cut out a dress with three sleeves, I swear."

Betta giggled. "I don't use a pattern. I just think how it should go, measure and cut. The dress sort of makes itself."

Torey finished putting on her makeup and digested this new information slowly. Were everyone and everything here other than they seemed? "Where do you get your ideas for the clothes, then?"

"Oh, I look at all the movie magazines and the posters. I even use ideas from the statues and paintings in the museum."

Torey gathered up a handful of pencils and a sketchbook. "In other words, you design the clothes. That is a valuable talent. There are several important Italian designers who are women right now."

"I never thought about it, Torey." Betta actually blushed. "I only want to make clothes for myself and my children someday."

A dark green Alfa was parked at the curb, the driver watching the street scene and smoking a small, thin cigar. There was little doubt it was Andrea. She had not expected to see him this soon, only a few days after the dinner. It was not that Torey hadn't thought of him—she had even made a few unsatisfactory sketches from memory—but somehow she had assumed his schedule would keep him at a safe distance. Thinking time and breathing space, her father used to say, will save fools from themselves.

"We're not late," Betta said to him immediately. "Not very late, anyway."

"It's perfectly all right, *cara*," he replied, kissing Betta's cheeks, "when a man has to wait for such a sight. You look marvelous and totally grown-up. And, Mrs. Gardner, it's wonderful to see you again."

"So formal, Mr. Scarpi?" Torey smiled at the pompous accent he affected. "I thought we were past that stage."

"Dear lady, this is going to be a very high-class tour. The help is not permitted familiarity with the patrons."

They set off on a meandering course across the city. Betta gave a short but highly accurate description of each church, old building and fresco, showing a full knowledge of all the major influences on the ancient city. Each place they visited was magnificent, even if sometimes neglected and dusty, but Torey found it hard to work up the enthusiasm to sketch them. Instead, it was the people around them who captured her attention. She wanted to set their faces down on paper.

Andrea said little for most of the morning. He corrected Betta's facts when they were inaccurate or pointed out a subtle detail here and there. Torey was acutely conscious of being watched by him, even measured somehow, and it annoyed her.

It seemed that every available inch of Palermo was filled. There were no spacious courtyards, parks, piazzas and wide boulevards as there were in Rome. The thready, narrow streets were all festooned with their banners of daily wash, and tiny jungles sprang up in areas Torey would have thought couldn't hold a window box. As the three of them strolled, ragged children, old shuffling men, laughing housewives and shoppers of all ages flowed around them. It became exhausting to get from one street to the next with the constant press of bodies. Andrea moved her skillfully out of the way of jostling, whistling bystanders, taking her arm and steering her easily.

Torey wanted to say *Don't stand this close* to him, but it seemed foolish and she didn't. Europeans always stood closer to each other in ordinary conversation than Americans; it didn't mean a thing, Paola once assured her, and she'd gotten used to it in time. Until today. The proximity of his face and body was very disturbing, making her lose track of Betta's careful speeches. When he took her arm up and down the steep cathedral steps, he kept his hands on her far longer than was absolutely necessary. His legs moved against hers over and over.

"Enough churches for today, Betta, and enough monuments forever," Andrea announced. "Torey is beginning to wilt in the sun and I want some ice cream. You run over to that *gelato* stand and let us relax a few minutes."

They sat down on a stone bench. Torey quickly sketched a scruffy urchin playing in the public fountain and a woman kneeling at a street-corner shrine, who seemed oblivious to the mass of bodies moving around her.

Andrea watched her work in silence for a few minutes and then asked, "Have you started painting yet? Betta tells me you have almost filled your rooms with drawings."

"No," admitted Torey, closing the pad. "I have been happy just to store up all these ideas. I haven't worked—I mean really worked—in such a long time, it's a little like starting over from the beginning."

"Then you should be happy," Andrea said, stretching lazily, "because it's a rare chance to start new, reborn to life. You should feel eager and see everything with a child's eyes. Do you?"

"I'm not a child," she said, shading her eyes in the white glare to see him. "And when I'm happy, unlike a child, I know the feeling will not last forever."

Betta brought them dripping cones and prevented any further serious discussion. She wanted to tell them both, in lurid detail, all about a movie she had seen. Torey had suffered through enough low-budget Italian films to know what the appeal was for Elizabetta. Love was always "the thunderbolt" that Sicilians sang about and celebrated. Betta, no doubt, believed in it with a religious fervor and wanted confirmation of its existence.

Torey listened with patience until Betta reached the part where the hero, having escaped prison and his love's outraged family who numbered in the hundreds, was scaling a mountain in the driving rain to see her once more.

"Good grief, Betta," she moaned, and held her head as if it ached, "I can't believe you thought it was so good."

Betta sighed. "It wasn't good, it was great, Torey. So sad, so beautiful."

"I'm sure it was," Torey laughed, "but I don't

think it was love. It sure doesn't sound like a very natural or comfortable relationship. If he was kissing her all the time, it was probably because they had nothing to talk about."

Andrea lit up another cigar and chuckled.

"Well?" asked Torey, appealing to him to help her out. "Are you going to sit there and let this child think some man has to rob a bank, climb an active volcano and fight off hordes of crazy relatives just to prove he loves her? Betta will spend the rest of her life looking for the John Wayne of Sicily."

Andrea waved the cigar in a gesture of dismissal. "It wasn't a volcano, only a tiny mountain. No hot lava to worry about! And Betta already knows she's worthy of all those deeds being done for her any day of the week."

Betta threw her skinny arms around him and kissed his face countless times.

"Betta," he said finally, "please go wash your hands and face in the fountain. You're sticky all over from the *gelato*. Then I'll climb the volcano for you."

As Betta skipped away singing, Torey tried to take him to task. "I was being serious and you know it! What kind of silly notions do you want her to hold on to?"

"I was being serious, too," he said. "If love is such a 'natural and comfortable relationship,' why do people have to work so damned hard at it? You made it sound incredibly dull—like washing the floors and falling asleep."

When they had studied in Rome, Paola had confided that Jon and Torey looked and acted as if they had been married twenty years, not two. At that time, she had thought it was meant as a compliment.

"Let's go, Betta," Andrea yelled. "If you don't mind, I'd like to make one stop on the way home, Torey. I have to pick up a gift at a jewelry store near here. I'm sure Betta won't mind shopping."

The store was clearly one of the finer places in Palermo. The owner bowed and hovered over them like a magpie in his rusty black suit. The negotiations between Andrea and the man were somewhat lengthy, so Torey and Betta admired all the beautiful items and played "If I had all the lire in the world."

Torey spotted a gold ring that tempted her sorely. It was a unique piece without question. There was a strange swivel setting which allowed the small gold coin to be moved, displaying a sheaf of wheat on one side and the magnificent head of a woman on the other. The design was simple and strong and, despite its obvious antiquity, looked very modern.

"You have exquisite taste, signora," said the clerk. "This is Aphrodite of the Sea. The coin was struck right here in Sicily by the Greeks to honor her."

Torey smiled and reluctantly returned the ring to him. "It is beautiful but far beyond my means."

She bought a red coral horn on a gold chain when the clerk swore it warded off evil and surprised Betta with a pair of tiny star earrings, delicate and feminine. She actually said, "Pretty things for pretty girls," before she realized who she was quoting.

Betta squealed and kissed her, twisting around to

get a clear view of herself in the mirror. She insisted on thanking Torey profusely even after Andrea had finished and they had left the shop, wandering away from further temptation.

"Oh, no," wailed Betta, just as they reached the Alfa. "Andrea, we didn't take Torey to the Capuchin Convent, and it was marked in red."

"No more churches," reminded Torey. "We can always see it another day."

"But I didn't want to go into the chapel," explained Betta. "I wanted you to see the chambers and go down to visit the sleeping ones. There are eight thousand mummies, no, Andrea?"

A nausea swept over Torey and she swayed, one hand clutching the car door. The thought of a gallery of phantoms evoked her worst nightmares.

"Victoria, are you all right?" Andrea saw the sudden paleness under her tan and the unsteady step she took. He coiled one arm protectively around her waist and felt her tremble against his body.

"I'm fine, really," she said. "I think it was too much sun for one day."

"I told you, Betta," he announced lightly, "we were not the best tour guides in Palermo. I better stick to building bridges." His face, however, was concerned and thoughtful.

"No, don't say that!" Torey protested. "I loved the sights, and Betta was as good as any professional guide. I have to admit Palermo can wear a person down, though. There is almost too much happening all around on every street."

Before Andrea had turned the key off in the

ignition, Betta had bolted from the Alfa and blown them kisses. She rushed into the apartment, eager to show off her gift from Torey.

"I'll walk you upstairs," Andrea insisted. "I promised Benedetto and one of his school friends I'd take them to dinner tonight."

"It was a lovely day, thanks to you and Betta."

Torey offered him her hand at the top of the stairs. She hoped he would forego the formal, meaningless kiss and settle for a handshake. How Italian men relished the effect the old-fashioned kiss had on women, particularly foreign ones!

Andrea gently took her fingers but slid his hand to her elbow and abruptly pulled her closer. From this distance he could enjoy the green of her eyes, the freshness of her perfume, and feel the heat of her body. When she turned her head to one side to deny him her mouth, he saw a pulse beat in her throat and pressed his lips lightly to that spot. He put both his hands on her waist and drew her to him easily.

There was a moment when the electric space between them closed and some circuit was completed. Torey felt unsure and unready but not unwilling to savor the sensation of being close to him. He turned and left her quickly, making her wonder if the embrace had really happened.

She threw her purse onto the couch and kicked her shoes off somewhere in the corner. Adding the sketches from the day, she sorted through all the work. Many of the ideas were good and would need only a little development before she started to paint. Others had the old quality of flatness and tightness she longed to break away from; these she dropped into the wastebasket.

As if exorcising a devil, Torey tried a simple drawing of Andrea's face. The line was good, the subtle shadowing of his deep-set eyes under the heavy arched brows pleased her, but an element was missing. The real strength in his features, including the perfect cut of his nose and mouth, had changed into cruel features. The scar across his eyebrow did not look mocking or striking, merely satanic.

As she put the paper aside, she had the distinct feeling of teetering on a cliff edge. Instead of stepping backward to safety, the insane desire to step off into space possessed her. It was a strong, nameless feeling and it tingled into the ends of her fingers. Her body suddenly recreated the feeling of him against her, and a sudden heat flared inside her. Deliberately she began to work and shut out any further thought of him.

The sky outside darkened gradually to pearl-gray and mauve before she stopped to scrounge something to eat. She found she had little appetite and wasn't particularly tired—a bad sign. A long, rambling letter to Paola about the past week only gave her a hand cramp, but she finished it, picked out six or seven of the best sketches and stuffed everything into a large envelope.

If Torey tried to sleep now, she was aware that the dreams would undoubtedly come and disturb the relative peace she had attained. Rather than chance it, she showered and put on a russet suede jacket and skirt, her latest extravagance. She thought if she walked to the harbor, a long walk, she might find a place to eat and be able to sleep when she got back. It was one way to insure she needn't take any of the small white tablets. Solitary walks had helped in Rome; there had been nights when she'd covered miles and miles, pausing only to chat with a tired woman watching the moon rise over the Vatican or to buy a hot *cappuccino* for one of the wrinkled pensioners who haunted the large piazzas.

Peppina knocked and let herself into the apartment, carrying a plate of cheese and grapes. "How nice you look," she exclaimed. "Betta will drool all over the leather, so don't sit next to her tonight."

"I'm not coming down for a visit," Torey said. "I think I'll go out for a while. Betta can copy the suit another time. I have a letter to mail to Paola."

"Not now! It's dark out, and he's coming back later for coffee."

"Who?" asked Torey in the blandest tone possible.

"Garibaldi! Who do you think, woman? Andrea told me he would be back about ten o'clock—after he took Benedetto back to school." She scratched at her cheek in confusion. "What is it? Didn't you have a nice day?"

"I had a lovely day," Torey reassured her. "I'd just rather be alone for a while, and I like to walk."

Peppina clucked her tongue. "You've been alone long enough, no? Surely you know he is coming here to see you. Even an American—forgive me for saying this—couldn't be so silly as to believe a man would find me and my wild children as interesting as you!"

"Look, Peppina." She tried hard not to get exasperated at the constant probing. "Andrea Scarpi is a very nice, very attractive man, but frankly, I am not looking for an . . . involvement."

"Who needs to look? But if it finds you?" She gave an eloquent shrug of her shoulders. "He's a man, you're a woman . . ."

"I'd noticed," muttered Torey, picking up her letter.

"Exactly my point, *cara,* and he's noticed you. Betta told me how he looked at you when you were busy copying little angels in your book or peering at some old statue. 'Like he will eat her up.' Her very words."

Torey locked eyes with Peppina and put every ounce of conviction she could muster into her voice. "Very flattering, I'm sure, and very observant of Betta, who looks for romance on every corner, but I prefer not to be devoured. I came here for a very short stay, to paint and think, and maybe to get myself on the track."

"You don't know Andrea," Peppina said sadly. "He isn't the kind of man who has to look for women; they seek him out. In the last few years, he rarely shows much interest in any one woman."

"You're right," agreed Torey, eager to get out. "I don't know the man and I probably won't. Please, don't meddle!"

Peppina threw her hands up in total disgust. "Fine, do it your way. Like Paola, you are a modern, stubborn woman. You would make a fine Sicilian being this obstinate!"

Without bothering to reply, Torey set off for the

harbor, relishing the cooler breezes on her face and the faint tang of salt and fish in her nostrils. She walked quickly through the virtually deserted streets and saw that very few places were still open. A middle-aged or elderly man occasionally passed her, walking off the effects of a large dinner. A street child played here and there and eyed her carefully. She had not been so silly as to take her purse with her; she was not an innocent in Italy. Here, as well as in Rome, boys practiced the fine art of grabbing purses and packages and then melting into the shadows.

The winds from the sea moved the smaller boats up and down among the larger ships and freighters. Torey propped her elbows on the rough seawall and watched the bobbing lights move, the waves slapping hulls, and lost herself in the deep quiet of the darkness. Jon had often kidded her about the hours she spent at the lakefront in Chicago watching the vessels load and unload, the sailboats gliding in colorful flocks in regattas. Since she couldn't run away to sea, she had said, although the idea was tempting, she'd settle for her second-best fantasy and become a stock car driver.

She turned around on the low concrete barrier and let the wind hit her face, spreading her hair in back and lifting it off her damp neck. It was akin to that feeling she had loved as she drove to the Art Institute so long ago with the radio blaring and the back of their old station wagon rattling with stacks of canvases. The wind would hit her face and rush through her hair. And sometimes she would sing in her off-key, throaty voice when the feeling, wild and free, bubbled in her blood.

But no more. Not since the night Jon died. She could still hear echoes of them shouting at each other and see his face contorted with fury at her. *"How can I work with your constant chatter, the radio blaring, the telephone and these lousy neighbors?"* And she had finally lost control and asked him when the last time was he had painted anything —anything at all—even a wall. Echoes of the door slamming as he left, wild with anger. The police had told her how very fast he'd been driving when he'd lost control of the car. The rational, thinking part of her understood when everyone insisted she need not feel guilty, and yet Torey hadn't driven since that night—or wanted to. But sometimes, especially lately, she found herself missing the free, familiar feeling.

The air was getting colder. Her teeth were chattering and she had gooseflesh under the jacket so she started through the small, dark square off the waterfront. A door swung open, nearly knocking her down, and two young men stumbled into her path, arguing loudly with each other. They walked ahead of her, crossing and recrossing the deserted square. At the corner they paused to hiss at each other in dialect and the shorter, more muscular of the two propped himself against the wall to deliver a final word. Suddenly, Torey knew they'd spotted her because their conversation abruptly stopped.

She passed them, ignoring the flowery compliments and loud smacking sounds. The men tried to outdo each other in style and volume. She was unperturbed; it was an accepted part of Italian life and had to be ignored. There had even been times in Rome when she'd laughed after an ardent admirer, getting no reaction, had turned to the very next woman, a stout matron dragging a screaming child, and used the very same phrases. It was a show of virility for other men, not a serious gesture.

One of the pair stumbled into her and grabbed her arm. He implored her to come with him in a stream of wine-soaked words. This was not part of the custom. Torey checked the rising panic in herself and stayed calm. If she screamed, she wondered, would anyone come into the square? Palermo was not Rome; it was becoming clearer by the second.

"Vittoria?" His voice was unmistakable, heavy with authority and undisguised anger. A car door popped open and a figure stepped out.

"Get in here, please," he said across the gloomy square. Andrea walked to within ten feet of where she was standing, still held by the drunk. "Now, Vittoria!"

Her name, Italianized or not, never sounded so good. She was ashamed at the wave of relief that washed over her. It was childish, dependent and weak, but she was relieved.

"Her husband," moaned the drunk, and he dropped her arm as if she had caught fire. The two men hurried off unsteadily, still loudly discussing her physical attributes.

"I gave you more credit for worldliness," Andrea said, opening the door for her. "If you insist on strolling alone at night in Palermo, I don't think you'll be pleased at what you find." He glanced over at her before he turned the ignition key. Torey had sunk into the leather seat and sighed, but clearly she was not the hysterical type.

"No, I'm not pleased at being mistaken for a whore. I'm just another foolish tourist looking for peace and quiet. Now I suppose I'll get a Scarpi lecture to put a finishing touch on the evening."

He spoke in a gentler tone. "Peppina was very upset when I got there. She thought you were only joking about walking alone, and then, when you didn't get back right away—"

"I don't mean to cast aspersions on the glory of your Sicily," Torey interrupted, "but if you have an extra, I'd like to borrow a *lupara*."

Her reference to the famous short-barreled gun for wolf hunting made him laugh. She was shaken but not too distraught to joke, and he liked that. In fact, the more glimpses he got of the mind resting inside her beautiful head, the more Andrea was intrigued with her. Tonight he saw the lioness again, sleek and lithe.

"You really are too soft-looking a woman to have such a sharp tongue," he scolded, and parked near a small bar. "Since I made the wild, successful ride to save your virtue and, incidentally, missed coffee with Peppina, I think it only fair you should reward me."

Torey looked directly into his hooded, enigmatic eyes. "I don't know. I suppose a drink might be payment enough for facing street-corner bullies, but remember, it isn't like climbing a volcano in a windstorm."

"A driving rain," corrected Andrea, leading her into the smoke-filled room.

The interior was drab and decorated with a jumble of old boxing posters and a few unsteady tables. There were only three other customers, all male laborers. Whether he had picked the place to gauge her reaction or there was simply no other place to go in the quiet city, Torey was careful not to make any comment.

The tiny table they sat at forced their legs together in an intimate tangle. When Andrea asked what she wanted to drink, she asked for a *caffè corretto*. She hoped the strong brandied coffee, a favorite of workingmen, might bolster her strength.

Andrea's eyes sparkled with a dangerous blue light and he ordered them doubles from a sleepy barman. "You probably are feeling a little shaky, no? Still, I wasn't aware lady artists drank with truck drivers. You are a surprising woman, Vittoria."

"I just know and like a lot of different people," Torey said candidly. "You look right at home yourself, although"—she gestured at a poster—"I'd bet you only boxed at university."

"A little, yes." It was obvious he didn't want to talk about himself. "As I was saying, you are not like other American women I've met."

"And you know thousands?"

"Thankfully, no. The few I've seen in Sicily put too much on their faces and too little on their bodies in public. They can make a certain high, shrill sound as they squeak about the heat, the flies, the quaintness and the terrific bargains." Andrea mimicked the voice Torey had heard in the bar off the market to perfection.

"And Italian men?" She couldn't resist her chance. "A lot of puffed-up roosters strutting in silky suits and crowing about their barnyard prowess to any dusty little hen who wanders by!"

"You left out the part about how we all boast of having voices like nightingales," he added with a grin.

Her laugh was rich and throaty. The dim light of the bar glinted copper and brass in her hair, and the sudden transformation of her face into such a soft vibrancy made his drink hard to swallow. He wondered if Torey had any notion of how captivating she was, or if her distance and disinterest was only a pose to catch a man off-guard.

She began to tell him the story of a conversation she'd had with a lawyer at Paola's. Torey explained how serious and boring this impassioned man was. He seemed every bit as staid and reserved as Roberto Vizzini, and he had poured his priceless advice into her numb ear.

"Suddenly he grabbed both my hands, Andrea, and burst into an aria from *Aida*. At the top of his lungs. And he gave a very creditable, if somewhat unexpected, performance!" The anecdote made her giggle and she couldn't stop, reliving her total shock and remembering how the other guests had merely stood around, listening politely, as if the man were announcing the latest soccer scores.

Andrea confided, "My roommate in college once seriously threatened to strangle me if I ever sang before breakfast again." He ordered two more drinks, loathe to destroy the new easy mood between them.

"Is that where you learned English?"

"First I studied in Milan and then went to London for a while. I learned English, engineering and a taste for fine clothes, but nothing to mend my Sicilian manners." There was no trace of apology in his voice, merely a statement of fact.

Torey began to regret not eating dinner, feeling the effect of the brandy. Her knees touched his in a slight, shifting erotic dance, and tonight she knew the spreading warmth was not whiskey or wine. Her pulse rate was faster and her mouth drier. It was very easy to speculate on what kind of lover this man would be, to wonder how gentle or forceful he was. She became achingly aware of how very long it had been since she had touched a man's body and heard the whisper of flesh moving against flesh.

"I think we'd better go back now," she said. "The effects of the evening and the drinks are catching up to me. I'm really not much of a drinker."

There was more to it than that and Andrea knew it. Back in the car, she toyed nervously with her ring and looked out the window. Her mood was as subdued now as it had been open a few minutes before. When they reached via Emma, he did not offer to walk upstairs with her.

"I won't be back in Palermo for four or five days, Torey," he said quietly. "I have to drive to Jato tonight, but I want to see you when I get back."

"I'm sure you will if you come to Peppina's,"

Torey replied with a false casualness that rang hollow even to her.

"I'm not sure. You weren't very eager to see me tonight, were you? I think your little walk was to avoid me."

She refused to answer, irritated at him and herself.

"Listen carefully," he ordered, and turned her by the shoulders until she was forced to look at him. "I don't, contrary to what you may think, force women into bed. I like to know them, to have them know me, and I like to be invited. When I come back from Jato, I'd like you to tell me who you are so distrustful of. Who is it who frightens you the most, me or yourself, Torey?"

Torey left the car without another word or a backward glance, but she couldn't put his question out of her mind. It was a toss-up, she finally decided. Beyond all reason and good sense, she wanted him. He made her feel alive again and she was enjoying the rediscovery of her needs, buried for so long. But though her body was eager for him, the blood pumping an insistent message, she knew how dangerous an affair would be, how it might hurt afterward to be alone once more.

Chapter Four

Peppina pounded on Torey's door with a growing sense of righteousness. It was Sunday, and if her guest would not go to Mass, she would not be allowed to ruin the day by working again from dawn to dusk. Peppina had given her solemn word to Paola Vizzini that no harm would come to a guest under her roof.

Yawning and stretching like a cat, Torey let her in. There was coffee brewing, but Peppina saw no sign of substantial food on the table. This was something to be corrected; the American woman was thin—too thin—already. It amazed Peppina how thick non-Sicilians were on matters of survival, how slow to learn what it took to thrive in a hard, unrelenting world.

Every inch of wall space was filled with sketches. The landlady surveyed the scenes and faces, noting one of Andrea in particular, but she offered no comment. She simply knew what she knew.

"I thought you might go to Montebello and relax on the beach today," Peppina suggested. "If you like, take Betta with you and give her a good day as well. She thinks of you as some magical creature sent to transform her as in some fairy story."

Torey smiled at the notion. "Cinderella? Sleeping Beauty? It's a nice idea, though, and I'll take the boys too, if you don't mind."

"Mind?" Peppina barked. "Mind? An hour of quiet is a gift from God. Gino, bless him, and I would sit as silent as two mice in our front room until very late, just to have a minute to talk without one of them crying in my ear or crawling on his lap. We used to wonder what it would be like when they finally grew up and left us in peace. But now, of course, I dread to think about them growing."

"They are growing," Torey insisted, "and they'll have to leave sometime." Leaving home was one of the hardest moments in her life. Her parents, particularly her father, had made it very painful.

"They are my life," Peppina said flatly. "I live only for them, and if they were all to go, I believe I would dry up and blow out to sea. Luckily, I don't think it will happen"—she lowered her voice conspiratorially—"because of the signs at their births."

When Torey asked what she meant, Peppina explained the custom of offering each newborn a tray.

The child's choice of salt, bread, wine or a rose predicted the baby's future. Her tone was sure and confident in the old folk magic.

"Aldo touched bread first and now he is in Agrigento learning a business; bread signifies labor. Only Gian-Carlo touched salt, the sea, so he may be the one who leaves Sicily. Beppo, that greedy one, put out both hands and touched bread and wine. We thought that meant his work would be of a higher order. Perhaps he will go into the church! Betta? She was so frail when she was born, we worried she wouldn't last the night, but she grabbed for a rose and wouldn't give it up."

Torey realized Peppina had perfect faith in the system and decided not to say anything offensive. She did ask what the rose was supposed to mean and was told that Betta was destined to reach for beauty in life. "Like you, *cara.*"

Torey tidied up the room, pushing the small easel aside. Her first attempts at painting had been less than successful. A day at the beach sounded like a good change. She was bone tired, almost exhausted. Her old insomnia had plagued her the last few nights, and this morning before dawn she had had disturbing, fitful dreams. Andrea had figured in them somehow, but Torey couldn't remember the dreams with any clarity. Four days? Five days? Would he be back today?

"I'll take them on the bus. I don't have a swimsuit but I can walk and sun myself. I promise I won't even take a sketchbook or a pencil. Tell them to get their suits and let's go."

Peppina's mouth dropped open in shock at the

notion. "Taking off your clothes outside is an open invitation to illness, Victoria. I know, the crazy visitors parade up and down in less than underwear, but it is positively unhealthy. Let the children play in the shallows only, please."

Montebello was not crowded; it was still early for the great influx of tourists, and few natives enjoyed the long, pale gold strips of sand. The two boys raced madly around, throwing wet clots of sand on each other and tormenting Betta when she scolded them. Torey watched Gian-Carlo splashing in the small waves and trying hard to catch a disinterested seabird. For most of the day, Betta sat pensively at the water's edge, her arms locked tightly around her knees.

The day slipped by, lazy and filled with the children's sounds. Torey loved the feel of sand under her feet. She was sorry to have to round them up and drag all three, protesting, back to a stifling bus. Beppo promptly fell asleep on her shoulder, reeking of tar and ripe fish.

"It was great," Torey reported to Peppina. "After I go up and take a nap and clean up, I can start fresh on a canvas."

Peppina was kissing and hugging the boys with a fervor usually reserved for prodigal sons. They managed to squirm away and escape to the street, grabbing raw vegetables she was chopping for fennel soup.

When she reached her apartment, Torey fell heavily on the couch and into a deep sleep. She struggled awake a few times when a dream threatened or the noises outside were too loud, but each time she fell back asleep instantly. One of the old nightmare visions overcame her suddenly and she heard a woman's voice screaming in terror. From past experience, she realized it was her own voice.

Her eyes flew open and Andrea was leaning over her with concern creasing a deep V between the dark wings of his eyebrows. Torey sat up quickly, bathed in a sweat that had dampened her hair and ran in thin rivulets between her breasts. Unsure if he was real or part of the dream, she stared pleadingly at his face. Her chest heaved with the effort to breathe, and her mouth moved but no sound came out.

"It's all right now," Andrea said softly. "It was a dream, just a dream. Sit still a minute and don't try to talk." He wet a dish towel at the sink and brought it over to her. Her hands shook so badly when she reached for it that he wiped her face and brow gently. "It's over. Just a dream."

She nodded and pressed the wet cloth to her face, calmed by the clean scent of linen and soap.

"I was downstairs and we all heard you scream. Perhaps a thief or a plumber?" When she didn't look up or respond to the humor, he stroked back the hair fallen around her face. "That bad, eh?"

She answered through clenched teeth. "I've had worse. I'll be fine in a minute." Gratefully she took the glass of cold water he offered and let it ease the constriction in her throat.

Andrea walked over to the balcony and stood looking out over the street. A muscle along his jaw twitched; his broad shoulder lifted and stretched the fabric of his shirt across his back. He held the yellowed lace of a curtain, clenched it into a fist and let it drop at his side.

In a more subdued tone than Torey had ever heard him use, he said, "I've had experience with such dreams myself. Even now, but not often, the old, bad things haunt me. But a dream is not life."

When he turned back to the room, she was sitting rigidly on the couch, crying. Her gray-green eyes were wide open and unblinking. The tears slipped silver down her face to her chin and dropped off onto her rose-pink blouse, leaving dark red splotches.

"Hold me. Please, Andrea, hold me." Torey had to force the words out painfully.

In three long strides he reached the couch and gathered her into the circle of his arms. He pressed her head to his shoulder and she moved, like a child searching for comfort, into the curve between his arm and chest. Andrea brushed the damp tendrils of hair from her wet, flushed cheeks and stroked the hollows of her face with strong, gentle fingers. The warmth and closeness of his body reassured her she was not dreaming.

Torey whispered to him, "I want so desperately to run away from the past. I'd try any escape that really worked. I'm just not strong enough. I've tried, and I'm not."

"Do you believe that?" he asked. "How can you hold on to such nonsense here?" His hand touched her left breast lightly. His mouth met hers in the gentlest contact and stayed there, tasting the saltiness of tears. His lips brushed her wet cheeks, drying them with his warm breath.

"Rescuing me must be getting monotonous," she said in an unsteady voice full of apology. Torey hid her face against the brown, warm skin of his neck.

Andrea's arms tightened and he ran soothing hands over her back. "Monotonous is not a word I think of when I think of you," he said.

Then his mouth found hers and was less gentle in another kiss. This time his lips and tongue demanded a response and his fingers cupped her breast, not soothing but tantalizing her.

"Please," pleaded Torey against his mouth, uncertain of whether she meant "please don't" or "please do." She was passive, totally vulnerable.

Andrea could have lifted her and taken her completely, proving with his body that she belonged with someone living, not a ghost. But he realized it would have been something done out of weakness, not choice or strength, and he found the idea distasteful. He released his grip reluctantly.

"I'll wait downstairs for you," he suggested. "Let's go out, walk a bit and get something to eat."

Torey moved mechanically through the apartment, drained of emotion. Her reflection in the mirror showed hollow eyes and pale lips; she applied her makeup as heavily as she dared without looking clownish. Her hands had steadied as if they belonged to someone else. And she found herself thinking how wonderful it had felt to have strong arms close around her and to hear the dull, steady sound of a heart under her ear.

"At least you don't spend hours getting ready," he commented nonchalantly and flipped the cigar toward the street.

They walked silently toward the piazza Pretoria, with Torey hurrying to keep up with his longer, purposeful strides. The harbor wind cooled and revived her. They passed the magnificent fountain dominating the square without slowing to admire it. Torey glanced at the massive writhing torsos of men and women in flowing marble. The work, which glorified the human form, seemed so alien in this almost puritanical place.

"Have you seen it lighted after dark?" Andrea asked, following her backward gaze.

"No. I wanted to, but remember, I have it on good authority not to walk around after dark alone."

"Let's walk back this way then. Under the lights the figures seem alive through some trick of optical illusion. It's very effective," he explained, lacing his fingers through hers.

They chatted about sculpture and other safe, impersonal topics. By mutual agreement, they avoided any subject that might evoke the earlier scene. Andrea took her to a small restaurant with huge dinners better suited to a crew of hungry stevedores. Torey labored valiantly over her *spaghetti chi sardi* when Andrea insisted that fresh sardines healed twenty ailments, including chronic indigestion.

"If I eat all this, I'll *have* chronic indigestion," Torey moaned.

"You like food but you don't eat much," he drawled, motioning the waiter to take her plate. "Do you want to starve yourself for a thin body only other women admire?"

"Don't you dare start badgering me," she said,

only half kidding. "I've heard the 'poor children in China' story for the last time. I still won't eat succotash!"

He looked so bewildered she imitated her mother's singsong voice and, in English, said, "Victoria Anne, eat everything on that plate. Don't you know there are children starving in China?"

He gave her a laugh of understanding and admitted, "I never heard that one, but then, I really was starving on the streets in Messina. Did you ever eat your what-you-call-it?"

"Good grief, yes! Every wrinkled lima bean, until one day I realized that whether I ate it or not, poor Mei-Ling wasn't going to get any."

His offhanded reference to his own childhood had stunned her. He carried himself like a prince and spoke with such educated surety; Andrea was a brilliant, confident man with an important position, and yet, in one brief comment, she knew he had been a boy exactly like those who pawed through the garbage of Palermo. The questions in her eyes could not be avoided.

"I am a bastard, the son of a Messina prostitute. I was always dirty and hungry and I did whatever was necessary to live." A small wave of his hand meant not to press for details. "It's a common enough story. Thousands of boys live as I did in Palermo, Naples, Rome. I'm sure you've seen them. The worst part was in winter, curling up in doorways or over a grating to sleep."

Torey had heard the thin tenors and sopranos of boys singing in the streets. They would weave a two-word song into a piercing, intricate melody. The words haunted her; they sang *"Ho fame"* over and over. "I'm hungry." She thought she could hear an echo of their song now, watching his handsome, angular face in the ivory light of the candle. Why would he open this dark and secret part of his life to her? It was plain Andrea was not the kind of man who shared confidences easily.

"There was a storekeeper," he continued, "whose name isn't important. He caught me stealing shoes from him. I was always getting caught because I was such a poor thief. This man had four children of his own, but he believed that soup can always be thinned. He made me keep the books for the shop and he fed me, bought me clothes, forced me into going to school. Only after I graduated from Milan did he call the note due. He wanted two promises."

The espresso in her cup was ice cold. Torey found she couldn't shift her eyes from his and chance interrupting his story.

"No matter where I went to study, no matter what job offers I got, he asked me to work here in Sicily. And I had to swear on my honor I would return his gifts to me to at least one other person. It hardly seemed unreasonable for giving me a good life." His face might have been carved in stone; there was no trace of emotion in his tone or his eyes as he finished. "His name was Scarpi, incidentally. It seemed fitting to take it."

Andrea had revealed too much of himself, and he regretted it even as he told her the story. It seemed weak to him, as if he wanted sympathy. He had spoken hoping to help her. To survive, a person had to be tough and not give up. He wanted her to know there was hope and help. Andrea was ready to give her aid and comfort, but she must have the will to fight for herself.

Torey finished the meal in silence, now seeing the scar on his eyebrow as the sole outward sign of that early life. But there were scars inside this man, too, and she had seen them when he spoke.

"Shall we go?" he asked suddenly. Without waiting for her answer, he helped her out of the chair.

His firm grip sent a now familiar current of warmth through her flesh deep into her body. She felt subtly different and slightly disoriented tonight. It was as if she had turned a well-known street corner and found herself in a strange city.

A leisurely pace brought them back to the Pretoria fountain. Andrea was involved in explaining the dam project at Jato and his hope it would put twenty-eight thousand acres under irrigation soon. He was enthused, talking expansively about the possibility of the poor farmland growing rich as it had been centuries before.

The pale marble glowed under soft illumination, suffusing the twisted figures with life. Cold stone breasts seemed to warm in the light and the ropes of muscle running down the powerful loins of a male pulsed with effort. He strained for a lover who eluded him by mere inches. How sad, Torey thought. He was condemned to reach for her forever while a couple entwined nearby, clinging together in blissful fulfillment. The fortunate woman had her head flung back, hair flowing in looped marble coils, while her mate pressed himself to her in endless joy.

Torey shuddered from more than the evening breeze.

Andrea put his jacket around her shoulders immediately. "I'll take you for a cognac to warm you. Or do you want to get back to the apartment?"

"The apartment," she said firmly. "I feel lazy and torpid from all the food."

"I'm sure it will do you good. I have another remedy for you and I'm prescribing it. There's only a week's work left for me at Jato and I promised Benedetto a short trip when I'm done. I think you are about ready for a change of scene; could you leave Palermo for a country outing?"

Her arm tingled where he held it, and her mouth recalled the feel of his lips on her earlier. The prospect of being with him thrilled her.

"I'm more than ready," Torey said. "I'm eager!" But it wasn't only a day away from the city she wanted.

He held her fast and she did not turn away. When he lowered a fierce, more determined mouth to hers, all his earlier gentleness was gone and Andrea let her feel the pressure of his lips and the demand of his body. Torey didn't struggle or protest but let her own mouth part, admitting the hard probe of his tongue. He savored the taste of her, the softness of her slim body pliant against his. He took his mouth from hers very slowly.

"I asked you a question a few days ago," he reminded her, low against her ear. "Do you remember?"

Part of her wanted to lie and pretend it had been

of so little consequence that she had given it no thought. It was dangerous to let him probe deeply into her emotions. He aroused feelings in her she had put away.

"Me. The answer is me," she said almost inaudibly. "Does that confession satisfy you?"

"It's really not important whether it pleases or satisfies me. I happen to agree. You are frightened and distrustful of yourself, even more than you are of me. The next problem, of course, is how will you deal with yourself? Will you keep running away or try to conquer it?"

"Don't analyze me, please," Torey cautioned him. "I paid a small fortune to professionals for that kind of help for a solid year. All I ended up with were some prescriptions for sleeping pills, a great book on artistic blocks, and few stomach-cramping insights."

He ran his fingers through her hair and hugged her. "What kind of insights?"

"Delicious bits of wisdom doctors offer their patients to gobble. They looked good and tasted good and made perfect sense up here." She tapped her forehead. "But when I swallowed them, they didn't fit my insides. They are all still rattling around in there, little indigestible jewels. Or maybe it's the sardines."

Andrea smiled in the dark. "You are a fascinating creature, Vittoria. You can see the most subtle shadow on a child's face, and yet you trip over mountains in the middle of the road. There is a beautiful young woman outside and an old, ugly ogre hiding inside you, making you miserable." He tapped the same place on her forehead.

"OK," Torey whispered. "I'll evict the ogre and try to rent the space to someone nicer."

"By next week," he said, "if not sooner."

The days in early June heated up rapidly. Soon the hot winds would sweep over the coast and vacationers would invade the sea towns and fishing villages, occupied in July and deserted by September. Torey had planned to get back to Rome before the exodus began. By *ferragosto*—August 15—even the big cities would be empty. Only the hardiest and poorest stayed in Rome. Paola and Roberto had discussed their plans to force her to some cool grotto with them.

The week had gone well. Torey worked daily on her paintings. The sun's new strength made her eyes water and dance with red spots. She ate more, finding a new appetite with the demands of the work and tempted by the wonderful produce and seafood of the huge market. Betta had haunted the third floor to watch her paint during the long, hot afternoons. They talked for hours; Torey used the girl as a model frequently, and Betta loved the chance to pour out the thousand and one miseries of an adolescent.

When Torey heard the girl, it was a faint record of her past. Through Betta it was easy to relive the wild feeling that she could do anything in life, and the grim moments when everything seemed impossible. Betta talked endlessly of her hopes, her secret dreams, while lifting her porcelain face into the streams of sunlight and holding another pose.

". . . or I could take my designs to a big store in

the north and see if they would hire me. In five more years, Torey, I will be nineteen and Andrea would only be forty. If he waited to marry me, I would be a wife and a mother and a great designer like Simonetta all at once!" Elizabetta arched her white swan's neck to ease a muscle spasm.

"Benedetto would be thirteen, wouldn't he? You might find that a problem, little momma. Why don't you just wait and meet lots of men before you choose?" Torey looked up and smiled, her hand poised over the canvas. Mentally she counted the days past. Tomorrow.

"I know Benedetto might be difficult for some women to love, like Niccola, but not for me. I love him already and he likes us all, so . . ." She shrugged and lost the pose entirely. "It would be just perfect."

Torey went over and rearranged her model, placing the girl's hands back in her lap and tilting her head so her hair, freed of the usual braids, waved around her face.

"Was Niccola Andrea's wife?" asked Torey, disgusted at her own curiosity and willingness to pump Betta for information.

"Oh, no," laughed Betta. "She was going to marry Andrea three years ago. At least, everyone in Palermo thought so, including Mamma, and she didn't like Niccola."

"You mean, you all know this lady? Hold still a little longer, Betta. I can hear you even when you aren't looking at me."

Betta squirmed and resumed the pose. "Of course we met her. Andrea says we are his family, too. She was the most elegant lady I had ever seen, and her clothes . . ." She went on for a full five minutes describing a suit she had seen three years before.

"Let's take a break," Torey said. "So why didn't Andrea marry this rich, gorgeous *Palermitana?*" You idiot, you're asking for trouble, she told herself.

"I don't exactly know, but I was happy he didn't," exclaimed Betta, pear juice dripping down her chin. "She was too good to eat with us and thought us very common. She is the daughter of the man who owns the biggest department store here in Palermo. I guess that wasn't the real reason, though. She said she wouldn't have someone else's child, especially Benedetto, no matter what. And then, once I over-heard Mamma say that Niccola had told Andrea she wasn't going to live her life in Sicily. She married a French importer and lives like a movie star."

Torey had grabbed up a sheet of paper to make a quick study of the girl, a fiery-eyed child defending her hero and gorging herself on fruit. "That's it for today," Torey declared. "I'm going to clean up this mess and do nothing at all until tomorrow."

Her style had really changed, Torey noted. The obsession with faces and bodies continued, and she had painted almost no landscapes. A drawing of Gian-Carlo and Beppo wrestling on the floor made her laugh and she pinned it up. Then she fished two charcoal sketches from under the couch. The figures were drawn hastily from a vivid, erotic dream she'd had one night. Torey knew immediately who the faceless bodies belonged to and recalled saying a name she ardently hoped no one had heard. She could not bring herself to tear up the sketches, which were quite good, but she hid them under a stack of others.

"Victoria?" Peppina's voice could knock plaster down in the ancient building.

Torey went downstairs to "confer."

"In over three years," began Peppina, "a certain man has never once called me to say he'll be here on such and such a day. Now, I was told not to meddle and I won't. But this morning Scarpi called and said he would be here tonight for supper. He didn't say more than that, but I'm a Sicilian. He didn't just want me to make a favorite dish, I'm sure."

"Thanks, Peppina," Torey said. "I'll wash my hair as soon as I finish a corner or two I was painting on."

"I thought so," sniffed the landlady. "I know what I know. I'll make stuffed artichokes tonight and you'll love them."

The sound of Beppo and Gian-Carlo screaming at the arrival of the green Alfa carried all the way up to her room. She was still daubing at Betta's portrait and there wasn't time to wash her hands, much less shower and change from the paint-streaked jeans.

"Come on in," she called at the knock on the door.

"Will it bother you if I'm here while you work?" Andrea asked earnestly, framed in the doorway.

"Not at all," Torey said, waving him into the room. "Help yourself to something cold from the refrigerator. I'm covered with paint or I'd play hostess."

She waggled smudged fingers in his direction and grinned puckishly, wrinkling up her nose. Andrea smiled at the natural ease, the artless way she had about her beauty. It told him she didn't care overly much about her looks or calculate the effect she had on him. He watched her paint, moving in front of the canvas, reaching up to fill in an area, and her jeans stretched invitingly over hip and buttock.

"You've done quite a bit of work," he offered. "That is very good, but . . ."

"But what? Did Peppina register the usual complaints with you? She's been hounding me every day to take a walk or eat a whole roasted sheep or get more sleep."

"Too much work is almost as bad as no work at all. I was sent up here with very strict orders to get you ready for dinner. You must take breaks and watch your schedule or I think she'll spank you."

Torey made a derisive sound and started cleaning off the brushes. "You also seem to work hard, Andrea. Commuting all over the place and then helping here or leading guided tours of the city. She doesn't snap at you!"

He laughed. "She's worse with me than with you. You just haven't heard us fight yet. Besides, I might point out, I do take days off. But you?"

Torey put each brush in its particular place. "I had days off, weeks off, months off! For the past two years I accomplished exactly nothing. Now, everything I see I want to paint, and it's exhilarating and brand-new. Can't *you*, at least, understand? I've had all the time off I'll ever want."

Andrea came across the room to stand beside her and see the canvas. It was another portrait of Betta, this one capturing a sly, almost flirtatious look. The style was looser, more casual than anything else in the room. The harder Torey had worked, the easier it had become.

"Time off," commented Andrea, "is such an American concept. They seem so obsessed with time and other natural phenomena out of their control."

"Are we going to argue or duel with brushes at twenty paces?"

"I can think of a million things we could do," he said, "if only you will take a break."

"All right," Torey agreed, scrubbing her hands in the sink. She glanced back at him. "Name two and I'll take my choice."

"Here's my first choice."

Suddenly his voice was at her ear and his arms were turning her, tightening around her. Hands dripping, she faced him and realized she had wanted this kiss from the moment he had appeared in the doorway. He made a slow, hungry assault on her mouth, even drawing her lower lip between his teeth and lightly nibbling it. There was no way to stop him from taking the printed cotton scarf from her head or from burying his face in her hair.

"I had to know," he whispered, "if every kiss would be sweet as that first one."

"And is it?" Torey asked teasingly. She knew the answer by the tensing of his arms around her and the hard pressure of his body holding her hips against the sink.

"Don't play games," he said in a husky, growling command. "I'm not a schoolboy any longer, and you are not a shy, frightened girl. Tell me exactly what you want of me, Victoria, and I will try to please you." He held her face captive between his tanned hands and looked at her with eyes darkened by need.

"Tell me," he insisted.

The intensity of his arousal excited her wildly. She had enjoyed sex and never had been ashamed of her own needs and their fulfillment. But she was not bold and had never told a man how she wanted to be loved. This sudden new demand frightened her; her past experiences were easy, pleasant memories.

She moaned and pressed her lips to his throat, breathing in the slight trace of tobacco and talcum powder. The words were so simple in any language, but her mind was paralyzed and she couldn't form them into English or Italian.

"I have to know," Andrea said, "it's me you want. Torey, say my name. Just that, my name for a start. Then you will find it much easier to tell me what you want."

A sharp rap at the door made her start guiltily but he held her firmly. His arms stayed wound tightly around her.

"Andrea," she said into the fabric of his shirt, and felt him release her. "Who is it?" she called in a barely controlled voice.

"Dinner is ready, and Mamma told me to say 'No excuses' and wait for you!" Betta wondered at the long silence that greeted her and tapped again, harder.

Andrea swore horribly under his breath. "Dinner was my second choice," he muttered finally.

Torey, tucking in her blouse and running her

fingers through tangled hair, convulsed with laughter. The remark, delivered deadpan but with a wink, relieved her of the tension. He was so unpredictable, intense one minute and casual the next. The constant shift in him, his moods and temper, was attractive but also what she found to be the most dangerous aspect of him.

Chapter Five

The tiny leather-covered traveling alarm showed seven-thirty. Torey set it back on the floor. She had been awake since six, watching the sun crawl slowly over the ceiling and highlighting forms in the plaster cracks and stains. Mornings were good for thinking time and breathing space; she needed both. What's your rush? she asked herself.

There was a strong temptation to call off this outing. Andrea had said she wouldn't be able to resist Cefalu. It was a marvelous place, and the museum there contained an Antonello da Messina oil. But it wasn't any painting by an old master she had to resist. Be fair, she thought. He hasn't done anything you didn't want done. Being angry at him is healthier than sulking or feeling numb. And the painful questions he posed were the same ones she had balled up and stuck in the back closet of her mind.

Andrea had said they'd leave at eight o'clock, but Italian time, it might be later. After she dressed, Torey put a sweater, her wallet and a sketchbook in a straw basket. Munching on a roll, she peered over the balcony. The green Alfa was there, Andrea leaning against the fender watching Beppo play soccer.

The black slacks he was wearing made him look slimmer and even taller. The pale blue and black striped shirt echoed the striking combination of his eyes and hair. Jato's sun had deepened his tan to a burnished shade, and his high cheekbones were reddened with windburn. Even as she watched, he moved into the street and began to field Beppo's passes. Andrea was graceful and quick, running as easily and effortlessly as a boy himself. He shouted approval or encouragement after every shot.

"Good morning," Torey called to him, throwing the basket into the car. "I forgot anyone could be punctual in Italy. Sorry I kept you waiting."

"Another of my hidden virtues, *bella*," he said. Andrea fielded the ball one more time and called Beppo over. He kissed the little boy with the wonderful unselfconsciousness that men in Italy so frequently displayed. "My trains run on time, and we still have another passenger to pick up."

He ran his glance over her, as open as Torey had been furtive in her examination. The bright tangerine of her blouse may have helped, but her color was heightened and her face more relaxed than he remembered. She seemed to have grown lovelier in one week's absence.

"Palermo has not entirely disagreed with you," he announced. "Whatever it is, the sun, the people, the air of madness or your work, you really look like you've bloomed here."

Torey thanked him for the pretty compliment but added, "I can see why the bloom is short for women in places like Palermo. If I had to contend with living here everyday—all the people, all the problems—I'd probably wither and die in a few years."

"Are you very eager to get back to Rome?" He asked the question casually and tried not to let the answer mean too much.

"I miss Paola and Roberto more than I thought I would. I feel fairly secure that I could paint there now as well as I have here."

"That wasn't an answer to my question," Andrea insisted.

Torey didn't want to make a commitment to leave or stay longer. She only shrugged and indicated she didn't know and switched the topic to Cefalu.

"It's a small village about sixty-five kilometers west of the city. Until July or August, it's worth the trip."

"You mean, until the tourists spoil it?"

"Precisely, Vittoria," he said with a grin, "but you said it, not me." The car stopped in front of an enormous U-shaped building, pale yellow and ornamented with old florid stonework. "Here's Benedetto's school. Just wait here."

A tall nun in long habit appeared at the doors in the heart of the courtyard. She spotted Andrea striding up the walk and promptly disappeared. When she emerged again, she had a small boy in tow.

"Benedetto," Andrea called, and quickened his pace toward the odd pair.

The child tugged free of the sister's hand and ran forward with a curious, short-strided pace not unlike a shuffle. He covered a few yards and stopped, waiting expectantly.

"Come on, boy, we've got a long ride ahead of us," shouted Andrea. The two of them collided in a tangle of arms and legs. The nun waved briefly and vanished.

There was lots of giggling and writhing when Andrea carelessly dumped the boy into the car, but the second his thin, flailing arms touched Torey, Benedetto sat up quickly and reached out a tentative hand. His touch was a question.

She saw the black, curly hair, the red cheeks and upper lip glossed with a thin film of sweat, the delicate features. But the cloudy opaque eyes, large and wide, impacted on her most deeply. This child was blind and Torey felt her heart constrict.

Andrea touched the small hand lightly, gaining the boy's attention without a word. "This is Torey Gardner, my friend from America. She's an artist, Benedetto, and I was sure she'd enjoy Cefalu as much as we do."

Without a hesitation, the boy lifted both his hands to Torey's face and traced her features. Next, he took her hands in his own and touched them all over, lightly but thoroughly.

"You're not a sculptor," he said. "There isn't enough callous, although she keeps her nails short and her hands have more definition and muscle than most ladies. Are you a painter?"

Andrea smiled broadly. "This is Benedetto Scarpi, a bolt of lightning in blue shorts. I should warn you, Torey, he's only eight, but he has a way with women, or so the good sisters tell me."

"I think he's part Sherlock Holmes," Tory suggested. "I am a painter, Benedetto."

The boy chuckled in delight and said, "I like him, but Nero Wolfe is a better detective, you know. And I'd really rather be a famous criminal."

"They don't teach it at your school, and, I believe, it's not a hereditary trait," Andrea pointed out.

"Neither is charm, Papa," retorted the boy. "Do you like Sicily, Torey? I have never been to America, but Papa promised we would go there someday to see the capital, Disneyland."

"I hadn't heard they moved it from Washington, D.C.," gasped Torey, "but considering politics, the change might make sense." To her surprise, Benedetto enjoyed the joke as much as Andrea and they got into a lively discussion of American life.

The coast road twisted and turned. At every sudden dip, Benedetto let out a whoop of joy and continued his nonstop chatter. His precocity amused her, and Torey found his childish exuberance a delightful contrast. When Andrea asked him about his studies for the week, Benedetto dutifully reported on his progress with literature, mathematics, chess and Francesca. The child explained seriously, in an aside to Torey, that Francesca attended the girls' section of his school and he found her "very interesting."

"She likes me," he announced solemnly, "but she doesn't know it yet. I danced twice with her at Umberto's party."

"You are your father's son," quipped Torey, aiming the remark at Andrea. Her mind was focused on the child's mother. What kind of woman could have such a fine child and leave him? The boy was bright and beautiful, perhaps too much like Andrea for comfort, but who in her right mind would abandon him?

"You very obviously avoided the mention of English or science," Andrea pointed out. "As Sister Veronica will tell me sooner or later, I would prefer to hear about it now." He tried to sound stern, but it was so patently false that Benedetto only laughed.

"I'm hungry, Papa. What did you bring me to eat?"

"Check the glove compartment and keep up your strength as you tell me the bad news. English and science?"

Benedetto deftly extracted a bag of fresh fruit and sunflower seeds. He generously offered to share it with Torey and blissfully devoured two pears, an orange and what seemed to be pounds of black-purple grapes.

"Come on," persisted Andrea, taking one hand off the wheel to tickle the boy, "what about your other subjects?"

"You will have to ask Sister Veronica," muttered

Benedetto. "I'm not supposed to talk with my mouth full."

The countryside flew by in a plaid ribbon of green, brown and yellow. Torey watched the wind moving across the grasses, bending them from a lush emerald to a silvery sage tone. The sun warmed the gray and brown rocks and glanced off them with a dazzling white brilliance. Now and then the Alfa shot past a lone figure plodding patiently down the road; inevitably the person would straighten and stop to watch their passage and then continue on with slow steps. Andrea was forced to stop for a few minutes to allow a small herd of black goats to cross. The brown girl driving them stood on the roadside in complete awe while the wind whipped her faded dress across dirty knees.

"She might be right out of another century," Torey said half aloud.

The trip was like a journey back in time. Cefalu, nestled at the foot of its rocky cliff, appeared to have changed little of its medieval face. At the height of the season, Andrea explained, the crowds would arrive to use the beaches and Cefalu would look around in surprise, keeping quiet and serene, and wait until the tourists left it for things to go on as they always had. The town was still relatively safe, dozing peacefully in the sun.

"First let's walk around and Benedetto can give you a superb lecture, no charge." Andrea took the boy's hand and started to walk toward the old cathedral that dominated the town.

"Hey, wait a minute," protested Torey, annoyed

at the breezy, almost bullying control he had over every situation. "I need my sketching materials and you've locked the car."

"You need a complete break, like Benedetto, from work," he said. "We'll look around, eat at the *osteria* and take a swim before we leave."

"I don't have a suit! The famous doctor, Peppina Barbera, discouraged me from buying one and inviting some terrible disease. And I don't really think Cefalu is ready for nude beaches."

Andrea appeared to think about it. It was a lovely prospect. "I should have mentioned it earlier, *bella*, but it's not important. Benedetto can play with the hotel manager's son and we'll climb the cliffs to see the coastline. Palermo looks better from a safe distance."

Torey fought the feeling of irritation and petulance down. She didn't want to spoil the day, so they set off as a trio for the austere Norman church with the boy tugging impatiently at their hands.

It was hard to remember the boy was totally blind. He moved confidently and easily most of the time. When he did occasionally stumble, Andrea never rescued him. Once, in fact, a quick, restraining hand held Torey back when she started to help the boy on steep stone steps. Andrea wants him to do too much, she thought, no matter how self-confident and able the child is. And yet she was aware that she would be tempted to love and help the boy to distraction.

An old longing welled up and tightened her throat. Jon had argued that having children was for later. When their careers were established, they would have plenty of time. Paola had been writing

Torey frantic letters about this new doctor she was seeing. She and Roberto had suffered through two miscarriages and she was willing to do anything, and see anyone, to be able to carry a baby to term. Paola's mother, a very distinguished matron, had gone to a shrine to enlist higher powers for the same desired result—a new Vizzini. But Jon had adamantly insisted that there was time.

"What a memory you have," Torey complimented Benedetto, making him glow in the church's gloom. His description of the history of Gagini's tender Madonna and Child sculpture would have put a lot of art history professors to shame. Her heart was touched when the boy ran small, sensitive fingers over a marble fold of the Virgin's robe with obvious love.

"Torey, now you must describe the mosaics, please," begged Benedetto. "An artist will be able to give me the details so I can imagine them in my head."

She began a word picture of the Byzantine works, emphasizing the activities of the angels and saints, including the variety of colors and styles. Even Andrea listened raptly and let a smile play around the corners of his mouth. There was tenderness in his blue eyes, but Torey was too preoccupied with her verbal tapestry of Apostles and Patriarchs to notice. It was more than Andrea had hoped; Torey liked the boy, and Benedetto was warmer with her than with any woman Andrea could remember.

"*Fantastico, eh?* Papa, I could almost see Archangel Michael slashing evil with a sword of fire. Perhaps Torey should be a writer?"

"I sure hope I paint better than I write, Benedetto. Words have never been my strong point. That's more your Papa's gift than mine!"

Andrea took her hand, completely enfolding it in his. "Don't you believe her. She can use words like the Archangel wields his sword."

It wasn't a particularly gentle touch from him, but her heart pounded and her mouth went dry. She ran the tip of her tongue across her lips and swallowed hard. There was nothing witty to say and no way to use words to combat this sensation.

They toured the tiny museum, and Torey had to talk about paintings for Benedetto until she could barely croak. The promised da Messina masterpiece was impressive. They stood for a long time before the painting while Torey told Benedetto about the man portrayed and how well the master painter captured the look of joyful animation in his subject's face.

"That's really the miracle of great art," Torey confided to the boy. "A painter can give us the same feeling of happiness and tell us so much about life in the fifteenth century at the same time. It's hard to communicate emotions without words. Time and place mean nothing when someone sees this work; I could stand here all day and just look."

"Can't we even go and eat?" begged Benedetto in real terror at the prospect.

They were still laughing about it when they reached the small hotel's patio. The food was good and Torey was ravenous, but she only tasted the first few mouthfuls. Every time Andrea passed her a dish, their fingers lingered together. His shoulder pressed her and his long legs brushed hers under the table, making her feel adolescent. Benedetto kept up the conversation between bites and covered every conceivable topic. He asked as many questions as Betta.

Outwardly Torey smiled and ate and answered about half his inquiries. Inwardly she had begun to regret the outing. There were approving looks from other diners at the little family scene they presented and part of her wished it were true. No matter how difficult Andrea was, she was undeniably drawn to him, and the boy could melt anyone's heart with his warmth. She didn't want to feel so involved.

An older boy, the manager's son, bounded into the dining area looking for them. The two boys greeted each other with a flurry of rib punches and embraces. Benedetto swore an extensive and meaningless oath that he would not swim immediately after eating and the two left like rockets for the beach. The older boy led Benedetto through the patio so casually that it was not obvious the younger boy was sightless.

"Is it safe to let him go in the water with just another child to watch?" Torey asked anxiously. "I mean, it's not a swimming pool, Andrea, and kids are so apt to be careless."

"No, it's not safe," he said, "but Benedetto is a boy like other boys. He wants to do everything in the world, safe or not, and I must encourage him. Mario is no fool, and the boys have spent several vacations together. Don't you be tempted to play Italian Mamma to him and get protective." He indicated by a stern look that the subject was closed.

Torey ignored the finality of his glance. "But maybe you should go too, Andrea. I'd feel better knowing he was safe."

"Yes, you like things to be safe, planned, reasonable. What's your favorite? Content. Life is not like that, you know."

She was not going to be intimidated by him. Her anger at the slap at her made her lash out. "Why didn't you bother to mention Benedetto's blindness? Was that some test of me, too? Did you want to check my reaction?"

"Yes," he said, "since you ask. I've found that telling people about Benedetto before they meet him makes them treat him more like a blind boy, not merely a child who is blind. Can you understand the difference?"

The blunt honesty cooled some of her anger. "Yes, I think I do. It was a shock when I met him, but he's a very special and wonderful boy."

"He's tough, too, Vittoria, and I don't want him weakened by people, even if they are well-intentioned. He looks and can act like an angel when he wants to, but don't be fooled. The sisters tend to pamper him too much, as it is; it's a common failing of Italian women to raise weak sons. Benedetto needs a sharp, insightful mind and a steel resolve to survive. He can't be safe from the world."

"If an iron will is genetic, then you'll have no worries," she said, and got up quickly to avoid further argument.

The daylight was white and blinding. Voices from the beach carried thinly up to her; Mario was waving and Benedetto was calling to her, crouched near a massive sand castle they had built. From this distance, the boy was a miniature of Andrea: slender, long-limbed and washed with golden color.

"Caro, we'll be back in an hour," shouted Andrea. "Let's walk off the pasta, Vittoria, and see Palermo from where it can't touch us."

When Torey protested she'd be happy just sitting on the beach, he taunted her a little about hovering over Benedetto or being afraid of him. She wondered how her honesty would affect him if she admitted to being frightened of being alone with him, but she said nothing.

The promontory was very steep, but an old foot path ran crazily up one flank, a long trail but only difficult in spots. Andrea led most of the way, stopping to let her look back down at the shrinking town or offering her his hand at the narrower, nastier places. The heat on the rock face was dizzying and Torey felt winded by the climb. She muttered under her breath and gamely kept up. About fifty feet from the top, the trail actually smoothed out into a wide, easy path, and Andrea let her go first. She walked easily onto the wide, rocky plateau.

It was barren of trees and fell sharply away on the seaward side. Around them were scattered huge, crumbling sections of an ancient Norman castle and an even older Roman ruin. Waves of heat shimmered in the air above the sentinel stones and even the breeze felt like burning fingers on her face. The panorama was magnificent, but Torey didn't want to survey it immediately. She threw herself down in the cooler shadow of a wall and rested her head against the timeless strength of stone. Through her shut eyelids the sun glowed a dark red, and she had to wait for her ragged breathing to subside. The air smelled strangely of fresh hay. She could sense Andrea very close to her but she didn't look at him.

"Vittoria, look at me," he said thickly. "Open your eyes and look at me."

Eyes still tightly closed, she stirred restlessly against him. Her breathing, rapid and still labored, reminded him of another time in her apartment, when his kisses had elicited the same sound. Andrea wanted to block out the sound and listen instead to the sigh of the wind or the hiss of the distant waves below. He had told himself he only wanted her company today and no more; he would not allow himself more foolish pursuit. But she was lovely and he wanted to see her eyes, the color of the olive leaf.

Wordlessly, he ran the back of his fingers along her cheek and throat, resting in the hollow there. The shadow of his face over her turned the red light behind her eyelids a soft purple. His mouth touched her eyes in turn and drifted to her lips so gently she might have imagined it. Each kiss was sweet and more difficult to end. Torey began to return them, her silken lips suddenly turning hungry and answering him.

Andrea twined his fingers tightly into her hair and held her still, absolutely still. He wanted to drink all the sweetness of her mouth, devouring her and the warm flesh of her throat. His fingers pulled the buttons of her blouse open impatiently and found the soft flesh, without the restraint of a bra to slow him or give him time to reconsider.

A tremor of such fierce longing moved through

Torey, she felt weak and sick. Her arms reached up and held him tightly, feeling power in the muscles across his back. He made a sound, sigh and moan in one, and her hips arched up to ease the fullness of desire they shared. His hard body moved slowly against her, sending currents of sheer pleasure through her. His fingers trailed lightly to her breasts, and his thumb and forefinger raised taut, sensitive peaks that ached until his lips replaced one sensation with a keener, deeper one.

Torey trembled, caught up in his tender, skillful lovemaking, and tried not to think, not to struggle anymore. Her body was welcoming each caress and waiting impatiently for the next one; why must her mind sound its old, tired warnings? The past was gone and she wanted to float lazily, enjoying his urgency, and let these teasing, knowing touches carry her away. It was so good, so inevitable, so wrong.

His mouth moved more boldly on her, stirring a wild sea of desire. Each new kiss, moist and searing, was another tiny wave eroding her resistance. She tried to sit up, pushing ineffectually at the rounded strength of his shoulders as he buried his face in the warm, taut flesh of her midsection. When he drew away slightly, Torey thought fleetingly that he had understood her reluctance and sensed her fear, was honoring them despite her traitorous body's response.

"Don't," she pleaded weakly. She was as fearful that he would listen and stop as she was that he wouldn't.

Andrea's hands moved lightly but surely along the

length of her leg under the skirt until his fingers found the tight elastic borders of her panties. His touch was knowing, moving easily around and over the curves of her hips and thighs, at first stroking gently at the silken material. Then, suddenly, he was setting fire to satin skin, finding and pressing urgently at the fiery core of her womanhood. The tidal wave of need that flooded her made her moan and fall back helplessly. She could not protest or look at him, hating her own weakness and yet wanting to drown freely in this flood of pleasure washing away almost every thought.

It was glorious to explore the smooth heat of his skin, to touch the dynamic lines of his muscled chest sweeping down to a narrow waist and lean, hard thighs. How could she deny the aching throb in her body, neglected and deprived for so very long? A deep and savage instinct made her writhe against him, her legs parting slightly and the muscles along her inner thighs trembling, even as her mind tormented her with a fleeting and painful image of another time, another man.

"No," Torey cried in real desperation to Jon's sudden vision. She felt Andrea's body shudder, locked in her arms.

"Look at me," he begged in a husky voice. "Please, Torey, open your eyes!"

She could not obey him immediately. Her heart was slamming too painfully in her chest and she was lost somewhere between desire and terror. It was not Jon whose body pressed hers down so thrillingly. It was Andrea, who she wanted and feared. It was

Andrea, who had made her undeniably aware she was still alive and young and very hungry for him.

He groaned in some terrible pain. "I cannot love you, not like this." And the wonderful weight of his body left hers.

It hurt more than a slap in the face. The sun beat down on her exposed breasts, but Torey had become nerveless with an instant, complete cold. Her eyes were blinded with passion and unshed tears and the lids were too heavy to open. A roaring in her head was all that remained of the excitement in her veins, draining slowly; it was not the sound of waves breaking far below them. She could hardly focus on his tense, strained face.

"It seems you were right this time," he said sadly. "We should not have left Benedetto. I thought an hour alone wouldn't try me, but I was very wrong. Forgive me, *cara.*" One finger traced the curve of her swollen lower lip with infinite care and tenderness. But his other hand pulled the blouse closed over the whiteness of her skin.

She sat up and turned away from him, embarrassed. Torey pushed buttons through with numbed fingers. "I can't," she whispered softly. "I wanted you and I . . . I'm not ready, Andrea. Oh, God, I'm so torn and frightened. . . ."

"I still want you now, this very second," he answered in a voice thick with desire, "but it will be completely or not at all."

She got up slowly on unsteady legs and brushed the fine gray dust off herself. When she walked to the cliff edge, she had to cross her arms tightly across herself to hold the pain inside. "Time," she began, and faltered. "It's not enough time. I haven't been with anyone else since Jon. . . ." Her voice failed and she choked back a sob.

Andrea was silent for a very long time before he spoke.

"No, you are wrong, Vittoria. Perhaps we should not have come here alone. I am not as controlled as I like to think—another instance of Sicilian pride—but you are wrong now. I'll say it all even if you hate me for it. There's no more sense in telling only part of the truth, *cara,* because we can hardly be friends, much less lovers, on a foundation of lies.

"It is *too much time,* not too little. You were ready to love; your body was eager and willing. If the fire that has been smoldering for so long in you can be set and extinguished by any man, then I'm too proud to be that man and too big a fool. I want you to know it's *me* you want, *me,* without the memory of another man shadowing us."

He stood close behind her and touched her shoulders very lightly, dropping his voice to soften the impact of his words.

"Torey, you kept your eyes shut as tightly as possible. Was it me who was loving you? Was it someone I can't even compete with? I'll use charm, wit, silly jokes, my body or even my anger to win you, but I can't fight your phantom."

She swayed visibly under the weight of his words and seemed ready to step off into the empty space ahead of her. Andrea grabbed her and pulled her back into his arms. Her face was ashen and her eyes blazed with green fire, raw and uncensored.

"Be angry with me," he said roughly, fearful he had gone too far. "Believe me, your anger is easier to bear than your sadness or fear."

"How easy it must be for you to read my mind," she hissed. "You have a child to love you and the comfort of good, productive work. Whatever I had vanished two short years ago, and rebuilding a life isn't easy. What's your magic solution, Andrea?"

"There is no magic, perhaps," he answered, and took her cold hands in his. He lifted her left hand and held it up before her face. "I can't explain freedom to you when you still wear a sign that chains you to the past."

She covered the wedding ring protectively, defensively with her other hand. "I never suspected you were cruel," Torey managed to say. "Temperamental, stubborn and opinionated, yes, but cruel?"

"Am I cruel?" He looked out along the coastline to the wrinkled, moving sea. "Am I only imagining that your ghosts crowd in on us and overhear our conversations? Am I the one who is cruel to you?"

Her face closed and she didn't speak. She had wanted him, but suddenly he was asking too much and he wanted it too quickly.

"Fight me," he whispered. "Fight back. But don't keep running away." He pressed his face into the wild mane of hair blowing around her.

No other woman, except his mother, had cost him a moment's pain. He had always been so careful and completely prepared by his early life to take what came to him. Niccola's attempt to manipulate him, first by warmth and later with threats, had failed completely. She had suggested a "compromise" and he had laughed at her. Lovers compromised on everything, but not on love.

"I want to go back now," Torey said quietly. "You told Benedetto we wouldn't be long."

The descent was easier than the climb up. Andrea watched her walking gracefully beside him. She took his hand when he offered it to help her past a jagged boulder or a slick patch of rubble. But she did not look at him.

He told himself he was right, damnably right, not to take her, but the vision of her soft, willing body under him tortured him. Everything Torey offered was sweet; everything he offered her was bitter, or so it seemed. She seemed further from him than ever, and he, in his worship of honesty and pride, had certainly pushed her away when he'd wanted her closer. He coldly reminded himself he'd had nothing before and survived.

Torey grew fearful and tense as they approached the beach. Children were more perceptive to mood and his child probably more than others. She dreaded Benedetto's comment on the pervasive and deep silence between them, but the boy was happy, sunburned and sleepy. If he noticed anything amiss, he kept it to himself. Benedetto dressed, chatting with them about the wonders of the warm sea and shaking dunes of sand out of his clothes.

The late afternoon sun melted the countryside into pools of molten gold. The car's tires hummed in chorus with the cicadas as Andrea drove fast but very competently toward the city.

Torey taught Benedetto how to sing "The Bear Went Over the Mountain" and discussed the various methods of building sand castles with him. When he finally asked about the hike to the cliff, she described the view in a firm, noncommittal way. He raved enthusiastically about the gentle surf of Cefalu.

"Papa must take you with us to Trapani next time," Benedetto said, falling back against her. His cherub face was pink and hot with the sun's kisses. "We have our house there, and I like it better than any other place in the world. You could swim with me there, Torey, and I would even practice my English. Papa?" He waited to see what effect the bargain would have.

Andrea glanced over at the child resting on Torey's chest. The Gagini Madonna and Child couldn't rival the scene they presented; Benedetto looked young and hopeful while Torey's face was calm and attentive, tipped down to see his son. One arm was loosely curled around the boy. Deeply troubled, he stared at the road ahead.

"I think, little one, our trip to Trapani will have to wait a few more weeks. There's lots for me to do at Carboi, and then, if there's time, we'll go before the London conference. Torey would be welcome to go with us, but I think she'll be back in Rome before then. Vittoria?"

"I will be leaving very soon, Benedetto," she said, and stroked the hair from his forehead. "I have lots of things to do in Rome and people I must see. If I were staying, I'd like to see Trapani. That's where they catch all the tuna, isn't it?"

She chatted with the boy but she studied Andrea's profile. "What might have been" was now a cruel and impossible fantasy. Her anger was gone, but the expected sadness never came. She felt resigned and there was no point in spinning out stories of the future with Benedetto. Today was no beginning; it was, more likely, an ending. She decided to call Paola the next day and make plans to leave as soon as the work she'd started was done. It was not running away, she assured herself. It was the sane, reasonable, expected end of the trip, and it was agonizing.

She glanced down and found Benedetto had fallen asleep in mid-sentence. His perfect mouth, sculpted like Andrea's but sweeter, still hung slightly open. She tugged gently at Andrea's sleeve and he smiled. Their eyes locked above the boy.

"Isn't there anything they can do for his sight?" she whispered. "I've read recently about new surgeries, laser treatments."

"We've been to Milan, Rome, Paris, and twice I took him to London. I've been willing to try anything from lasers to Sicilian folk magic. I let Peppina and Betta take him to the shrine of Santa Barbara. Finally, I accepted what must be. The condition is complex, the result of neglect as an infant and also heredity. The boy's blindness is total and permanent."

He tried to sound unemotional, but Torey thought she detected a faint undercurrent of bitterness. Perhaps the philosopher found it hard to live his own advice at times. Heredity? The implications hit her hard and seemed to explain why there were no brothers or sisters for Benedetto. Women would be eager for Andrea, and he so obviously loved children—not only Benedetto, but Peppina's brood.

A stirring of pity ran through her, not for Benedetto, who was loved and fortunate in many ways, but for the strange, hard man who had lived through his own horrors to have to face more with his son.

And his pain would go on and on, she realized. The rigid set of his jaw, a muscle twitching, warned her of the strain he felt. She pried no further although she burned to ask about the boy's mother.

Andrea woke the boy when they arrived back at the school. Benedetto clung to Torey too tightly for such a brief acquaintance, burying his head in her blouse and hugging her almost painfully. She read it as a sign that Benedetto was not as mature as he first appeared in manner and conversation.

"Would you visit me or call me on the phone while Papa is in Carboi? I get so lonely . . . I hate when he has long trips," Benedetto whimpered.

She looked at Andrea for approval. He only shrugged his shoulders and spread his hands. It was clearly her decision.

"Yes, of course I will," Torey promised. "And after I leave, you can write to me in Rome—in English for practice."

For one horrible moment she thought the boy would cry and set her off. He kissed her manfully on both cheeks and said, "*Ciao*" in a reedy, small voice.

"And me?" Andrea asked, getting back in the car. "Have my Sicilian manners or the lack of them finally cast me into hell, like a Dante character? I hoped we might part friends, if not lovers. Will I see you after Carboi?"

"I don't think so," she replied, determined to be strong. "I really will be leaving soon. But we are friends, and that hasn't changed. I'd be a pretty poor artist if I never learned to take harsh criticism and bounce back, wouldn't I? I was angry and hurt today, sure, but I'll live!"

"Torey?" He touched her hand and held it.

She saw the message in his eyes but it wasn't clear. "Yes?"

"Nothing," he said finally.

When they arrived at her apartment, he was silent for a moment. "Take care of yourself and keep your promise to Benedetto, please. He's very taken with you."

She watched until the Alfa was lost in the tangle of traffic before she trudged upstairs. She felt drained. It was only sensible to get finished with the paintings and get out. He was the most attractive man she'd ever met, the most involving and exasperating. He had put her on an emotional roller coaster with a word and a lift of one split eyebrow, and now the ride was over. It hardly mattered anymore that he was so often right in his insights. Andrea was too much of a threat to the fragile hold she'd taken on her life. His kisses made her foolish and weak, and his words could shatter her into a hundred pieces. A man like Andrea could never offer her contentment!

Chapter Six

$\mathcal{T}$he constant tolling of bells reminded Torey it was Sunday. Nothing would be open in Palermo but churches and hospitals. Torey planned out her day, dull and quiet. When Betta visited after early Mass, she had news. Paola had called when Torey was in Cefalu and said she would call today about one o'clock.

We were always on the same wavelength, Torey thought. *I would call her from Chicago and find out she had just mailed me a letter. What will she make of this mess?*

"Mamma says you should come downstairs early to wait for the call. The phone lines have been terrible all week, and I wanted to show you some new material I have to make clothes."

"Fine," she agreed, "and I'll tell you all about the

paintings I'm finishing. I'm sorry I've been too busy to chitchat the last few days, but since I went to Cefalu, I've been working steadily."

"Was the trip nice?" asked Betta slyly.

"Let's say it was interesting and leave it at that. I enjoyed meeting Benedetto. The boy is exactly like Andrea in many ways."

Betta gave her a peculiar look and shrugged. Interesting? Betta had seen the look on Andrea's face the last night he was in Palermo and she had been pushed bodily out of the kitchen by Peppina. The girl hadn't missed the bottle of brandy Andrea had brought, and she had heard the "discussion" that followed. Peppina's voice had risen to glass-breaking levels, and Andrea's rumbles had shaken the framed photograph of her Papa. Interesting? Adults were interesting, all right.

By noon, the apartment was hot and airless. The ideas Torey had been working and reworking bored her. She took a quick shower, changed and ambled downstairs. Peppina was refereeing a major fight between Gian-Carlo and Beppo, making a large meal and braiding Betta's hair simultaneously. The noise level in their tiny apartment should have been illegal.

"I could come back in half an hour," Torey volunteered. It was impossible to imagine people living and thinking in such tumult. The din of Palermo, like this family chaos, was often overwhelming. Peppina had said they lived to fight and experience the very rawness of life. It was exhausting to watch, let alone live.

Peppina ended the argument by simply knuckling

the boys' heads in rapid succession, giving them money for ice cream and shooing them out. She finished Betta's hair with a flourish and assured Torey she was only too welcome. "You know I love to chat. Good talk keeps me going."

"I never met people who loved to talk or argue more," admitted Torey. "But mostly argue."

"No, we don't," insisted Peppina, proving the point.

"Well, it's getting too much for me, I suspect. I decided last week to go back to Rome as soon as I'm finished with a few more paintings."

"When? When are you going?" Peppina seemed genuinely distressed.

"Ten days, no more. I'm going to tell Paola when she calls."

"Will you take the job with her for Vizzini Fabrics?"

"Why not? It will be good money, and Rome has been like home to me." There was nothing in Chicago for her, that was certain. "I'll try to show the work I've done here in Rome. I'm very pleased with some of it."

Peppina sat down at the table and traced the pattern in the oilcloth with her finger, her mouth drawn into a tight knot. "You don't like . . . like it here, then?"

Torey hastily reassured her. "It isn't just a question of liking or not liking Palermo. I had some childish notion I could run away and be happy, a kind of Disneyland of the heart." She had to explain Disneyland to Peppina. "I'm seeing things differently and more clearly now. It isn't the place that matters as much as me. Andrea was right on target about that—I've carried the past on my back like a grieving turtle."

Peppina said, in rapid dialect, "It's not good to be alone. And it's not my place to tell you what to do . . ." But her look indicated she did know and was dying to tell. She looked more of a bird than ever, her head cocked to one side and the small black eyes snapping.

Torey waited, knowing the advice would be given. The strangest thing was that she felt receptive. A few months ago she would have laughed at the notion that someone might have the answers, but she had been changed by this place in small but significant ways.

Peppina forged ahead. "You really want to go back to Rome? For what? More loneliness? You and I both know your work is going well here. My children and I find something rare and special in you, and you are involved with people here."

There was no mistaking the look, the emphasis on the word *people*. Peppina meant Andrea.

"Things have gone well with the painting," Torey said, "but not with Andrea. It's been too fast, too out-of-hand. I'm not ready for pressures. I must still need time to sort my life out."

"Are you crazy?" shrieked Peppina. "Do you want a schedule for life? On Tuesday at three I will be ready to live! Until Friday next June I must stay apart from the world! You, of all people, should know better. An artist has times when the work is slow and difficult and he pushes on until it starts to go right. A picture can be fast or take years.

However long it takes, that's how long it takes. There is no right or wrong time for any of us. If you stay, Torey, I feel a masterpiece growing."

There was real affection and concern in her voice. It was also obvious to Torey that Peppina had thought it over carefully and had kept the speech ready for a while.

"There's lots of considerations," she tried to explain. "I'm almost at the end of my money." She found herself thinking of Jon's insurance settlement with less distaste than usual. She could write to her father and have it transferred. But she was sure she was leaving. It was foolish.

"Think about it and I know you will make the right choice," Peppina said. "Paola can help you, too. I spoke to her for a long time when you were away in Cefalu."

"I felt I knew you before I arrived," Torey confided. "Paola and Roberto still love to tell all their favorite Peppina stories. They have a great affection for you."

"I'll bet they do," grumbled Peppina, in mock disgust. "They tell all their wealthy friends about the mad woman from Sicily who worked for them for years, the woman who hung the laundry lines over the formal courtyard, doctored them with rhubarb syrup and knitted thick black wool socks for Paola every winter." She captured the Roman lilt to perfection and her imitation of the Vizzinis was like hearing a record.

Torey laughed and couldn't stop.

". . . and their Peppina went to church every morning for ten years and prayed that little Paola would find a decent husband. When she brought home Roberto, what did the crazy Peppina say? She screamed at love-sick Paola to never marry a lawyer. What kind of man makes a living with his mouth? He'll talk more than Paola and be incapable of fixing a toaster. I told her to marry a shoemaker, that's the ticket."

They both dissolved into wild, helpless laughter. Peppina was crying and hitting the table with the flat of her hand, recalling Paola's shocked surprise. Torey rubbed the stitch in her side and howled.

"Paola admits you were right." She gasped. "Poor Roberto can't even change a light bulb." Torey vividly recalled seeing him trying to reason out an approach to their ultramodern Swedish lamp.

The laughter continued a solid five minutes until the two women were completely weak and helpless. They settled down over a strong cup of coffee but every few minutes, one or the other would snicker and it would start again.

The call from Rome came through before Torey could compose herself. It wasn't easy to make arrangements to leave and explain how the trip had proved to be too much when she was still wheezing with laughter.

Paola luckily dominated the first few minutes with a detailed report on an old classmate from Chicago who'd passed through Rome for a few days. Paola was sure Torey would be gratified to learn that Alice, now Alys, had left husband number three and was illustrating shoes in a mail order catalogue. Roberto was fine; he was working on an enormous case for Fiat and commuting often to Milan to meet with the directors. He had also broken his little finger playing tennis and had reinjured the finger on the coffee table when Paola had made a "small" joke about his athletic prowess.

"But, *cara,* are *you* all right?" she finally asked. "Your voice sounds funny. These connections are atrocious!"

"It's really a long story. I'm going to leave here in about ten days. I've been thinking it was a mistake to come here but—"

"Didn't we try to warn you? Leave now and you'll be here in a few hours, Torey. I can have Roberto pick you up at Da Vinci."

"Paola, listen for once in your life! I said it may have been a mistake, but I have some paintings I want to finish before I go. Have you gotten the letters and the sketches I've been sending?"

"You sent me something in the Italian mail? Were they registered, marked express? Really, Torey, you know better than—"

"I want to finish one sentence, Paola. I sent everything registered and insured. See what you think, but I'm sure they're really good. I need your final seal of approval, and I want you to take them to old Viviano at the gallery and wave them under his nose. See if he's interested."

"All right, I understand. Are you having troubles with my sweet Peppina? I know her children can get underfoot."

"I adore Peppina and the children. You'd never recognize them after all this time. It's been more like visiting relatives than renting a studio. Do you remember the girl, Elizabetta? She seems to have a real talent and interest in designing fashions. She's very good at sewing."

"Don't tell me," sighed Paola. "You're adopting her! I knew it. A short stay in Palermo and you have your own reform society going. You are incorrigible, Torey."

"I'm not going to spend an hour on the phone explaining it all. The letters will get there eventually and you'll get the whole story. I mentioned Andrea Scarpi, and that's part of the reason— Stop squealing! No, I'm not having an affair. Its a complicated and strange situation. We spend a lot of time arguing with each other." She had to pause for breath.

"Thank the saints you've joined the living," Paola said, sounding as if she was accepting another designers' award. "I don't care if he's a short, dark Sicilian mole who sells lottery tickets. Roberto will be thrilled. I think you should stay a year and paint those adorable horses and carts. The trip doesn't sound like a mistake to me. Don't come back unless you're bored. We miss you terribly but what wonderful news!"

"You never listen," groaned Torey. "I said very distinctly *fighting*, not *loving*, Paola."

Static on the line almost obscured Paola's chuckle. "You still aren't an Italian, Torey. I suspect much more, and aren't I always right? Well, almost always. Roberto is the only human who makes no mistakes. I'll wait for the letters!"

After a quick good-bye, Torey hung up the phone feeling both confused and lighthearted. Did she say she was staying or leaving? She hadn't told Paola about Andrea's son or the mess at Cefalu. The notion of Andrea as a dark little mole was funny; what would Paola say if she had seen him the other day, tall and unbelievably handsome, exuding an air of undeniable virility? Stop it, she scolded herself, you're heading back into dangerous waters. Work, work, work, and leave with some dignity intact.

Betta dragged out bolt after bolt of material for Torey to look at and admire. She was still shy about showing her work, but once she became involved in a discussion of fashion, her face took on a confidence good to see. Torey admired the five dresses Betta had made for herself and a similar number of outfits for Peppina. Betta asked her for criticism of the work and the design, but she had to admit she wasn't really qualified as a judge. To her untrained eye, Torey saw nothing wrong; everything was meticulously put together and professionally finished. She told Betta she had bought clothes in expensive Roman boutiques that couldn't compare favorably with Betta's work, and she meant every word.

"What you need," Torey said, "is someone like Paola to look these over. She knows fabric and design, and I'm sure she'd look at anything you sent her in Rome."

"Do you really think so?" Betta seemed overwhelmed with the idea of such a famous person showing interest in a beginner's work.

"Paola has a lot to do with who buys her fabrics and how they are used; she doesn't just design fabric and sell it. Most of all, she has contacts in the business who could tell you how you could best use your talent."

Betta's eyes sparkled warmly as the dream took

shape. "I would want to make something special for her to see."

"This suit is very nice," said Torey, holding up a simple but elegantly cut black suit Peppina wore to church and on special occasions.

"No," said Betta with great feeling. "I'm going to make a dress just for you, and then you will model it when you go back to Rome."

Torey started to protest. She wasn't staying very long, she didn't want Betta to go to so much trouble, and the fabrics were too expensive. Elizabetta gave her a look straight out of the *Sicilian Handbook of Arguments*—firm, unwavering and final.

"All right," said Torey, "if it means that much to you. I love pretty clothes and I've never had a personal designer. But you must let me pay for the materials."

"It's not necessary," Betta insisted. "Andrea gave me money only last week for more fabric. You see, you are not the only one who likes my work, but you are my first real commission. That's the right word, isn't it?" Her chin was thrust out with pride and she glowed. Elizabetta looked older than fourteen at that minute.

I looked like that when I told my father I was taking the scholarship and going to the Art Institute, no matter what he wanted, Torey remembered. She recognized Betta's determination and hoped it would bring the girl what she wanted most. If only, she sighed inwardly, she doesn't marry too young or to someone who will dissolve the dream into a practical, sensible hobby, sewing for the children or the neighbors for extra money.

Elizabetta pulled out a length of incredibly silky material in a dark green and fingered it gently. "This for the basic dress," she said solemnly, "and this"— she opened a sheer tissue of pale gray and silver— "for over the dress. The style will be classical like a painting." Betta actually winked at Torey.

"You devil, you've been planning this for a while!" Torey was stunned. "These fabrics are fabulous and very dressy. I can't believe you see me that way."

"Absolutely. I want to create something so beautiful people will faint when you wear it." Betta threw herself on the floor and dramatically held her hand over her eyes. Now she looked exactly fourteen years old.

"Okay, Dior, when do we start?" asked Torey. "You'll have to arrange fittings around my painting schedule or I'll never finish in ten days."

They set up plans like two conspirators. Betta pulled out a tape measure and a piece of brown wrapping paper, taking down measurements Torey wasn't sure anyone used to make clothes. She cheerfully submitted because of the intense happiness on Betta's face.

Peppina watched them from the kitchen, lost in her own thoughts. She saw how very young Victoria looked when she smiled, how very different from the way she sometimes appeared. Peppina knew the pain she had glimpsed in Torey's eyes and wished a well-placed word could relieve it. But she had been told not to meddle and that left her only prayer. She decided another trip to church might be in order, to pray for Torey and for Andrea, as well. If he could

bend his pride as easily as he bent steel into bridges
. . . She shook her head and went back to cooking.

Torey worked steadily in her apartment from first
light until the room grayed and her eyes ached. The
fierce impetus to have concrete work when she left
led her on. She had to contend with frequent visits
from Peppina, who checked on her state of health
and made dire predictions which ended each discussion. She lost track of the days, laboring over the
growing number of canvases. If she ran into a
problem of color or composition, she simply
propped it against the wall and worked on another.

When she ventured downstairs, it was to call
Benedetto at school. The first time he heard her
voice, he crowed with delight and babbled so rapidly
he slipped into dialect. "I keep my promises," she
assured him when he begged her to call again. The
stark loneliness in his voice was unmistakable, and
she wanted to tell him she shared his feeling but,
thankfully, she managed to keep their conversations
light and silly.

Paola called twice more from Rome. Once, she
reported she had received the sketches and was off
to see Viviano that very day. She raved on about
Torey's work until Torey was actually embarrassed
and begged her to hang up. The second time, Paola
spent such long and pointless minutes rambling on
about Roman gossip that Torey asked her point-
blank if she was drunk.

"I'm worried," Paola had admitted. "Peppina told
me you are working too hard and eating too little

again. You know, you don't have to stay another minute!"

Torey had lost her temper and snapped that she would be back when she was finished and swore she was fine. She counted it as half a lie. It was true concerning the work. She was not fine when it came to thinking about "a certain person," as Peppina pointedly referred to Andrea.

Since he'd left, she had relived the day at Cefalu a hundred times or more. Her hands would be busy blocking in areas, filling in details of a face or a tiled roof, while her head replayed a far different scene. Sometimes she swore out loud in English to keep eavesdroppers from understanding. The memory still hurt, and she slapped paint on a scene of Norman ruins with a vengeance. He was arrogant, proud and stiff-necked, and all in all, he was right. She had to throw away the canvas when she punctured it with a brush in frustration.

After a while the hurt and humiliation had subsided into dull embarrassment. She found herself looking often at her silver wedding ring. Every time her hand moved in front of her face, the circle of olive leaves confronted her. Andrea had been right about a lot of things, but she kept the ring on. When she was ready, she would put it away in her jewelry case. Not yet.

The worst reminders of Cefalu came at night. She saw the faces of the two lovers meeting and moving together in her dreams. It was no longer a faceless, nameless lover who satisfied her in tormented, heated visions. It wasn't Jon's face or lips or hands trailing fire over her, making her say things she'd never said to a man. It was Andrea. She woke up exhausted in twisted, sweat-soaked sheets and forced herself back to work. Her mouth burned with remembered kisses.

"Torey, it's the phone . . . for you." Betta's voice was muffled through the door. "It's Andrea in Carboi. I know you're awake, so please, come down."

She ran to the phone, unconcerned with her unseemly haste. She wondered if she had become sillier than Betta, dreaming about movie stars, while pretending the days and nights hadn't been passing.

"Vittoria?"

How could he make the sound of her name so much like a caress, intimate and gentle? Torey saw Peppina staring at her and turned away, pressing herself against the wall for strength. Her knees felt unsteady.

"Is everything all right, Andrea? It's so late. . . ."

"I don't know if everything is all right," he said. "That's why I called, *cara.*" There was a pause. "I thought you might have left for Rome. Is your painting going well? Peppina sounded concerned."

"I'm pleased," she answered. "I've talked to Benedetto four or five times on the phone, and he sounds happy. I think little Francesca discovered his irresistible charm last week, but, of course, he misses you." She hesitated only a second. "I miss you too. I wish you were here with us." With me, she had wanted to say.

"Do you need a critic so badly?" He laughed and his voice seemed very close to her. "Don't misunderstand me, Torey. I'd be glad of any excuse to be there. Can you possibly stay in Palermo a few extra days? I'm trying to get all the plans done here, and I think I might be back Thursday."

"No—I don't know," she stammered. "I don't think . . . I really should . . ." Peppina was standing boldly in the doorway without making the slightest pretense of disinterest. Torey switched into English. "The chief reporter from the *Palermo Times* is listening, I'm afraid. I don't know about staying. Why do you ask?"

"I want to see you and talk to you before you go. I hate talking on the phone, Vittoria, and there are twenty men in this lobby waiting for a line. I'm not hanging up, though, until you say whether you'll wait or leave."

It was easy to visualize him standing there, all the strong, angular planes of his face composed and his voice stern and full of authority. He had not said exactly why he called or what he wanted to talk about, just posed another question for her to answer. The smart thing to do was to keep to her schedule and leave.

"I'll stay, Andrea. What is this all about? Are you sure you're all right?"

"*Now*," he said with clear emphasis. "Now I'm fine and anxious to get back. Give the children a kiss from me. I'll give you mine when I see you."

Her heart gave a double beat and slammed painfully against her ribs. It probably sounded to his audience like a tired businessman talking to his wife in Palermo. She wanted to tell him how much she wanted him with her, his arms around her and her face tilted up for his kiss. Torey wanted to be able to say how much she wanted him.

"I've thought about . . . what we talked about in Cefalu. Andrea, I really would like to talk some more soon." She glanced at Peppina who had started, inexplicably, to laugh and walk away.

"Talk?" he said softly. "Of course, we'll talk. Golden dreams, *bella*."

She stood there with the receiver clutched in her hand long after he'd hung up. It was infuriating to realize she was this light-headed from a mere phone call. He had the ability to affect her without being in the same room or even the same city. It had been stupid to agree to see him, knowing with what ease he could turn on a hidden switch in her and make her pulse pound, her body experience a surge of excitement. It was wonderful and heady and would make her departure more difficult.

"Coffee, maybe?" Peppina suggested blandly. "You are already down here so you might as well stop working and take a break."

"Thanks. I can take a few minutes, but I have to get back before the paints skin over."

"It's almost midnight," Peppina moaned, "and you look exhausted. I only hope the call wasn't bad news. Is Andrea okay?"

Torey had to laugh. "Very, very subtle of you, Peppina. Is Andrea okay? Didn't you ask him yourself when you answered the phone?"

Her landlady grinned engagingly and refused to answer.

Torey coaxed her, using the same wheedling voice Betta used so often. "Come on, you're dying to tell me something or ask me questions, aren't you? Neither of us will sleep tonight if you don't get your chance."

"Well, maybe I want to know why he called you in the middle of the night. Maybe not."

"He called to check and see if I was still in Palermo and if my work was going well and if I was all right. It was very sweet of him."

Peppina puffed out her cheeks and made a rude noise like a child. "Sure, sure. Do I look like a farm girl? You had to speak English with Andrea to tell him you're still here and so on. What else?"

Torey took a sip of coffee before she answered. "I told him I might stay for a few days more."

"Might?" The black-olive eyes bored through her.

"Okay, I will stay until he gets back from Carboi."

"And?"

Italians! thought Torey in despair. No people on earth can say one word and wring so much out of it or put so many meanings into it. Peppina said "and," and made it an entire volume. She didn't want to surrender completely and tell all.

"We want to talk. We had a few misunderstandings and a few harsh words and we'd like to part friends."

Peppina didn't even deign to say a word to express her disbelief. She simply folded her arms and twisted her lips in utter amazement.

"Now stop that," Torey insisted. "You may have some terrific scenarios in your head, Peppina, and if you enjoy them, fine. But it's not that way, and it can't be. I'm just not the 'thunderbolt' type, and Andrea certainly isn't! He's never committed himself to more than friendship, and I think I've explained my own feelings to you adequately. I need my work and friends and time and I need order in my life. I don't need a romance yet."

"The two of you are a prize pair," snarled Peppina. "He once sat there, right where you're sitting now, and drank a half bottle of brandy and told me the same words. 'I need my son,' and 'I need my work,' and 'I have enough obligations for any man,' amen. Just because I told him a man alone can't raise a child, even a strong and able one, while a sickly woman can raise ten babies without a man, God forbid."

Torey grimaced. "Peppina, that was cruel and unjust! Andrea is a wonderful father to Benedetto. And he is deeply involved in his work; it's a vital part of who he is."

"A child needs a woman to love him in a special way," Peppina said. "Presumably if Benedetto had a mother, he wouldn't grow up as pigheaded and stubborn as Andrea."

"Betta told me you didn't like Niccola, the department store princess, and now it sounds as if you advised him to marry her. I can't understand you at all, Peppina." Torey picked at the ends of a dish towel, wondering why she was defending Andrea so earnestly.

"Niccola Sanfelippo? Hah, not that cold-blooded cash register in fancy clothes! I was talking about real women—like us." Peppina snatched the towel away before Torey could shred it to pieces. "I offered to relieve him of the Barberas if we had become too heavy an obligation. He's done more than enough for this family, and I told him so!"

"Now you're the one who's talking crazy," Torey said. "You and the children are as much his family as Benedetto. He loves you."

"Yes, he does," agreed Peppina, nodding sagely. "And because he was drunk by that time he even said it straight out. Goats all over Sicily sprouted wings on such a miraculous occasion, I'm sure. What nonsense, drinking and fighting with me because you two had—what did you call them?—harsh words at Cefalu."

Torey got up from the table. "What he said makes sense to me, and I don't often agree with him. He was warning you not to meddle in his life, and I've told you the same thing, haven't I? There's no 'thunderbolt' of love for people like us, just hard work and friendship. Thanks for the coffee."

Peppina walked with her to the door, reminding her that Betta wanted to try her muslin mock-up of the dress tomorrow. Torey was ready to agree to anything to get back to work.

"Hey," Peppina yelled at her retreating figure, "ask Andrea about the *terremoto* when he gets back."

The earthquake? wondered Torey. Ask him about an earthquake? Her first impressions of Sicily were close to the truth. Everyone here was a little crazy.

Chapter Seven

She primed the huge expanse of her final canvas. Even the tedious job of applying a white undercoat was more enjoyable than she recalled. Torey surveyed the blank space and had to face the reality that it would be difficult to complete this in six days. At one time, she would have allowed herself six months. She asked Gian-Carlo and Beppo to roll the remaining canvas and have Peppina store it.

"Time to start working!" she exclaimed, sweating in the afternoon heat that poured through the glass French doors. "This is it, the home stretch."

The boys were incredulous. They wondered what all the drawing, painting, hours of stretching and tacking and priming were, if not work. They left her, whispering and giggling to each other.

Six days! She had to scheme to get enough illumination for the large painting, enlisting the boys to scrounge lamps from the neighbors. It was possible to work long into the night with artificial lighting. It was easier to catnap on the couch, fully clothed. She forced herself to take breaks, eating while standing at the refrigerator and staring at the sections she'd just done. When the apartment got unbearably stuffy and hot, Torey took a quick shower and was back at work in minutes.

"Mamma," mumbled Betta through a mouthful of straight pins, "will be up later to threaten and scream at you." She took a tuck in the bodice Torey was trying on. "She's very angry with you and with me. She said I caught your . . . I forget the word, because I'm down there sewing and sewing while you are up here painting, painting, painting."

"Obsession?" guessed Torey. She was trying to conjure a mental picture of Benedetto for the foreground of the picture.

"That's the word," nodded Betta. "I'll be back later to check on the length of the skirt."

"The door is unlocked," Torey reminded her. "You can come in any time the lights are on. Betta, is today Monday?"

"Tuesday," said Betta. "You just asked me that before."

All right, Torey conceded mentally to Peppina, this may be obsession. I'll take a break. She phoned Benedetto's school and talked at length with the mother superior. Her careful explanation of who she was, what she wanted and how she knew Benedetto was regarded with open suspicion. The nun only said she would consider the request and return her call in an hour.

Torey dressed in her best gray slacks and the beautiful Vizzini print blouse of scarlet, gray and black, which felt as if amorous spiders had spun it. With makeup on for the first time in days, she grabbed her sketchbook and left the via Emma at a brisk pace.

She didn't hesitate in front of the ominous iron gate across the courtyard but pushed it open with authority and knocked at the wooden door. When a lanky sister appeared, she showed Torey to the foyer and disappeared. The mother superior came out, plump but not jolly, at the intrusion.

"Mrs. Gardner?" The older nun gave her a highly critical look.

I should have worn the black skirt, thought Torey. "Yes, Mother, I'm the friend of Mr. Scarpi. I thought I would come over rather than wait for your—" she began, sure and composed, but a small figure darted out of the hall and tackled her tightly around the waist, knocking the wind out of her.

"Torey," he shrilled. "I knew it was you. I told Sister Veronica you smell like carnations."

Torey got a laugh out of his greeting, his novel method of identification and the shocked look on the two nuns' faces. "You are lucky, Sherlock, that I wore the right perfume today."

The mother superior's English was excellent but strongly accented. "What exactly did you want with the boy, Mrs. Gardner? We always try not to disturb the children unduly, and he has classroom obligations."

"I understand your reservations perfectly," Torey said, "but I have been, as you know, talking with him on the phone and I did promise I would visit. Wouldn't it be possible to take him for a short walk and an ice nearby? I can have him back here whenever you wish."

"Please, please," begged Benedetto. "I'm sure Papa won't mind; he loves Torey very much, too."

His debatable choice of words and not very politic phrasing in front of the sisters made her wince mentally. She tried out what she hoped was a very winning, innocent smile.

"Mrs. Gardner," said the mother, drawing herself up, "we must be extremely careful these days. There are kidnappings and even worse of children from fine families. But I suppose . . ."

Torey and Benedetto marched out hand in hand, trying not to laugh and conscious of the stares on their backs.

"I feel like a criminal," Torey whispered out of the side of her mouth. It set the boy into a seizure of giggles, ending only when she crammed a lemon ice into his mouth.

"Fine families," snorted Benedetto. "Did you hear her say that?"

"Mother didn't mean you were related to the House of Savoy, you imp. She's worried and trying hard to take care of you." Torey took a bite of the ice he offered her.

"I like it when Papa takes care of me," Benedetto

said with fervor. "I hoped and hoped you would come to rescue me. I told Papa that on the phone, and he said you were too busy and not to expect a visit. But I knew you would come."

"I almost didn't make it," Torey said. "I have been busy, painting every single day and almost all night. I know, that's a bad excuse, but I lost track of the days since I started this one canvas. I came to ask you a favor, as a matter of fact, regarding the painting."

Benedetto laughed and slipped a sticky hand in hers. "You want *me* to tell you about a painting?"

Andrea had said it all. "I accept what is." The boy joked about his blindness in the same offhanded way Betta had mentioned death and Andrea his terrible childhood. Torey laughed too, finding it easy to accept what would have horrified and saddened her such a short time ago.

"My goodness, no! I didn't have a critique in mind. I need a sketch of you, if you'll pose. I want your face in the front of this painting." She described the scene of the canvas and how she wanted it to look when finished.

Benedetto listened with a grave air, asking his usual encyclopedia of questions, mature and perceptive. He even wanted to know what the painting was going to communicate, reminding Torey of what she had said about the da Messina oil.

"Well, I want it to show the aspirations and hopes of Sicily," she told him, "but not a realization of happiness, because that wouldn't be the truth. If I do it right, it won't be a sad picture."

"You sound like Papa," exclaimed the child. "He

always says our country is conquered but undefeated, poor in everything but spirit."

Torey talked him into another ice without difficulty and they strolled back toward the school. She posed him on a stone bench covered with whitened, eroded gargoyles. As she outlined his features, she talked to keep him attentive and still. He loved her anecdote about Beppo trying to taste the paints, unable to believe a rich tomato red or a spinach green would not have any flavor. He was interested in Betta's dressmaking and how secret the operation was, with no one, not even Torey, getting a peek at the final creation. Torey captured him in a striking three-quarter view, finely detailed down to the minute crease on his forehead—a perfect miniature of Andrea. Benedetto wiggled and scratched.

"You're a very handsome boy," she said, "and you look just like your Papa. In English we say 'the spit and image'—a little disgusting, but accurate. Of course, I never saw your mother; you may look like her as well."

Benedetto scowled fiercely, his expression changing to one of deep hatred. It was like Andrea's face in anger. Torey recoiled at the similarity of mercurial temper.

"Don't ever talk about her," he shouted. "I hate my mother."

"All right, *caro,* all right," she said. She felt his anger and pain acutely and realized she had touched something very deep in the boy. "I'm sorry I upset you, really I am. Relax your face and let's talk about something pleasant. Trapani? You told me how much you love it there."

He reverted to a smiling, happy little boy. "It is the best place on earth. The air smells so good I feel full like I'd just eaten a big meal. The fishing nets are rough and warm from the sun and we play all day on the beach. The sea comes up to our door, and Papa taught me how to swim there. He's a great swimmer with real medals from the university."

It explained perfectly Andrea's long, lean, muscled body. He had the smooth physique of a swimmer. But nothing, she decided, could explain the Sicilian mind. She should have listened when Andrea said the boy was tough; it was warranted by the blaze of hatred she had seen in him.

Benedetto warmed to the subject of Trapani. ". . . and Papa built our house himself with his own hands. It is perfectly safe from storms. Teresa lives in town, but she stays with us sometimes. She was my nurse when I was little, but of course I don't need her now."

"Of course not," murmured Torey as she put the final touches on the sketch. She had promised he wouldn't be late and they had only a few minutes left.

"Do I really look like Papa?" His reedy voice was plaintive.

The note of doubt made her stop and smile at the innocent beauty of his face. "Yes, in every way. I'll bet Andrea looked like your twin when he was eight."

"That's strange, isn't it?"

"No," she said. "Why should it be strange? My eyes are the same color my mother's are, and I have a nose just like my dad's, even to the little pushed in part on the very end."

"But he's not my real Papa," came the artless answer. His wide, cloudy eyes seemed to stare directly at her. She sat stunned. "Papa found me in Messina four years ago. He wouldn't have let me eat garbage if I were really his son. Now, he's my only Papa forever, he told me. Torey?"

The sudden sense of it flooded her and left her gasping. She put the puzzle of strange looks and remarks together with Andrea's story of his promises to the man who had helped him. It made her want to cry. "I didn't know," she managed to say.

"Torey, are you all right?" Benedetto made his way over to her and put his thin arms around her shoulders, even patting her gently as if she were the child.

She tried to assure him she was fine, explaining that working so hard made her weepy. She also said she was sad to think about leaving so soon.

"Then don't go. I don't want you to go," pleaded Benedetto.

"It isn't forever," she said. "I'll come back and visit you. When I'm in Rome, you might be able to come and see me."

"No," he insisted in a soprano imitation of Andrea's sternest tone. "I don't want that. I want you to stay here."

She felt utterly miserable, upset with herself for coming here and disturbing Benedetto. The fact that she had not meant to hurt him only made it, somehow, seem worse—a stupid blunder. She had thought only of her pleasure in seeing him once more, of sketching him, and not once of how he might react to her. But he's tough, she reminded herself and tried to believe it. Probably much tougher than she would ever be. She stood up slowly, holding him now.

"We have to go back, *caro*. I promised. I could call you before I leave."

He wouldn't talk to her at all. She kissed him good-bye gently on both cheeks while the nuns beamed at her. He was formal and polite, thanking her for the ices and shaking her hand, to the unabashed delight of the sisters.

She taped the new sketch of Benedetto to the wall as a reference point and mixed the flesh tones to block in his figure. That last look on his face, stricken and pleading, haunted her and bled away all the wild enthusiasm she had started the day with. She worked the next few days past the point of exhaustion, painting until she could hardly stand and had to drag herself to the couch for a few hours' rest.

"I'm not coming in," announced Peppina. She stood with her shoulders squared and arms folded tightly over her middle out in the hall.

"Fine," said Torey tersely. She sat up, groggy and cramped, and tried to remember where she was.

"We Sicilians don't like to get near mad people. We are afraid insanity is catching!" Peppina felt particularly feisty, having just won a terrific argument with Betta. She stormed into the room.

"That accounts for the high immigration rate," snapped Torey. "The sane ones must leave, because

I don't see a trace of mental health in anyone left here."

"You sound like a native yourself," countered Peppina. "I can't believe you are the same person who sat at my dinner table a few weeks ago and was so frightened by an argument."

Torey gingerly got up and rubbed her eyes. "I don't think after this trip I will be afraid of very much. I want to use your phone again. I have to try and talk to Benedetto at school."

"You see, you are crazy! You saw him two days ago and called him yesterday. I was absolutely right to call!" There was triumph in her tone.

"Who did you call?" Torey gave her a look she wouldn't have recognized in the mirror—a hard-eyed, accusing stare. "Who?"

"Paola. She made me responsible for you and I told her what has been going on here. Not eating, not sleeping, acting strangely! She will handle the matter herself, she said."

"If I didn't feel so damned awful," Torey shouted, "I'd chase you downstairs myself." But Peppina had fled in judicious retreat.

Torey spent the day running down to try unsuccessfully to get Benedetto on the phone. The school said he could not come to the phone, but she suspected he simply did not want to talk to her. Late in the afternoon, she gave up and curled on the couch. The painting was finished and she had anticipated feeling wonderful. Instead she was too tired to enjoy the end of her labor, too worried about Benedetto to even comprehend what she'd accomplished. And Paola? What had Peppina done? And

Andrea? What would his reaction be when he got back? She fell asleep, grateful to escape the confusion of her thoughts.

All the lights in her apartment were still on, forming pools of light on the floor and wall and glinting off the still-wet areas of the large canvas. Torey lay on the couch, mouth parted slightly and one hand thrown protectively over her eyes. Her hair was drawn back into a single, long braid like a child's, and she slept in her blue jeans, streaked with hand smears, and the white cotton shirt knotted tightly under her breasts. Her bare feet, narrow and high arched, were speckled with blue and green acrylic, and streaks of paint feathered her forearms. Andrea watched her sleeping, newspapers spread under her to protect Peppina's old couch from paint. That small evidence of thoughtfulness in the midst of obvious frenzy and disorder amused him.

He had counted twenty canvases—they were everywhere—and he moved quietly through the room, pausing to look at most of them carefully. Although her biggest canvas dominated one whole wall of the apartment, he waited until he had seen the others, knowing this was the one she had expended most of her energy and love on. It was an overwhelming view, and he was thankful he had not awakened her and that his first sight was private and unhurried.

The children dominated the picture: Peppina's three and Benedetto; and far in the background, a scrawny girl with a pale pink dress flattened across her knees by the wind herded goats. The fields were pure Sicily, with pulsing greens flowing into gold and ocher, broken here and there by the hard teeth of rocks thrust up from the earth. Betta was poised on a huge boulder, one leg dangling and the other knee bent gracefully for balance. She held a piece of embroidery in one hand, but her face was lifted to the sky with the same dreamy, lost quality Peppina had hit her for half a hundred times. Benedetto stood all alone in the foreground holding aloft a flaming sword like Michael, the Archangel, dressed in a schoolboy's blue shorts and sandals. Gian-Carlo and Beppo wrestled fiercely in the tall, bending grasses behind him, oblivious to any miracles he might perform.

Andrea's impulse was to wake Torey up, hold her and kiss her in celebration. He guessed the paintings were the best she'd ever done, and the final one was, in every way imaginable, a superb work. He bent over her and gently took her hand from her face. She stirred but didn't wake. Her skin had taken on a translucent quality, a pearliness, showing thin lines of blue vein at the temples, and pale lavender shadows hung under her closed eyes. There was strong evidence of strain and fatigue, but she seemed infinitely more lovely and desirable than she had at Cefalu.

There was no response to his light kiss or even the sound of her own name. Sliding one arm under her knees and one under her shoulders, he lifted her easily, allowing her head to fall against his chest.

"Is it really you, *caro?*" she muttered. "Andrea?"

The garbled words thrilled him. She spoke in

Italian, not English, and called him "dear one," called him by his name. She knew no ghost or dream held her but him.

"What is it?" he whispered, moving toward her bedroom.

"Put me down, I can walk. Where are you taking me?"

"I'm taking you to bed," he said.

She laughed, a sleepy, disbelieving sound. "I won't say no, Andrea, but I really ought to have a bath first." She chuckled when he put her down on the bedspread.

"I meant I'm putting you to bed—alone. It's after two in the morning and I just drove in from Carboi. I'm not in top form for lovemaking, *bella,* and you seem to be in a coma."

"The paintings," she said, trying to explain. "Did you see them?"

"They were hard to miss," he answered, and tugged at the zipper of her jeans. He worked them down over her hips, leaving only the narrow bikini panties on. Then he unknotted the shirt.

The brush of his fingers on her flesh made her shiver and she tried to wake up and focus her eyes. "Andrea, I have to tell you something. I . . . Benedetto . . ."

"I know all about Benedetto," he assured her. "That's why I drove straight in and I'll handle it. Sometimes, Vittoria, I wish you wore a bra." He pulled her arms out of the sleeves, admiring the pale gleam of her skin. She was totally unresisting, limp and drugged with sleep. It was too tempting to touch her.

"And I wish I needed one," she giggled. "A full, voluptuous lady for a Rubens, a Picasso . . ."

"If I were the painter, Torey, you would always be the model."

He touched his lips to the soft, gentle slope of her breasts, kissing each in turn. Her hands reached up and stroked his hair, her fingers reaching around his neck to draw him down to her. He took them away easily, kissing her hands, and stood up. He went to get a damp washrag before his resistance was completely shattered.

"A bath," she said as he scrubbed at the spatters on her arms and feet. "I remember saying a bath. Will you settle for a shower?"

"I won't settle," he answered. "When we make love, I don't want you asleep in my arms before we are finished. Now, don't be so difficult and get under the sheet."

The word *when* came through to her. He too shared her feeling of inevitability. The prospect warmed her as much as his hands tantalized her. She smiled, a secret contentment in the dark, and suddenly the whole miserable day came back in a rush.

"Oh, Andrea," she moaned. "I made a mess of everything. The visit with Benedetto, and Peppina thinks I've gone completely mad! She called Rome to have Paola come and get me, probably in a straitjacket of designer fabric. I was the one who wanted things simple and uninvolved and I've made a total mess."

He lay down beside her and brought her into the secure circle of his arms, stopping her protests with his mouth. A kiss was the most simple, direct way of dealing with her, although it had its own dangers. She clung to him, her body heating his through the thin linen, and her mouth gave back unguarded, unstinting pleasure. He was slow and unhurried, knowing there would be time later for a full discovery of her.

"Nothing is as terrible as you imagine," he told her finally. "The worst part is over, believe me, and you have won."

"Don't leave," she said, boldly. "Stay here with me tonight."

"Shush," he warned, holding a finger to her lips. "You forget where we are and you'll make me forget, if I'm not careful. Do you want word of my infamy and your dishonor spreading all over Palermo?" He laughed softly and kissed her again. "Peppina would be here with Gino's old gun in the morning."

But he held her and ran his hands gently over her back and shoulders until she fell asleep. Torey had almost forgotten the small, but wonderful satisfactions of hearing another heartbeat, slow and regular, under her ear, and sharing the warmth of another body, close and comforting.

Andrea was gone in the morning but the room still held the faintest trace of a citrus aftershave and the sheets next to her were wrinkled and creased. However dreamlike the night had seemed, she knew it was not a phantom, created out of loneliness and need. She had kissed and been held by Andrea.

Chapter Eight

*P*aola perched on the wooden table, swinging her shoes by thin straps and gaping openmouthed at the paintings. She had taken the early plane from Rome, but every artfully arranged curl of blond hair was perfect, her pale blue suit was spotless and crisp, and she looked as if she had just left for an hour's shopping.

After hugging and kissing each other, Torey asked, "Is Roberto waiting downstairs with chains to drag me back to Rome, or did he stay home and tend to business?"

"He's in Peppina's kitchen eating everything she puts under his nose. He thought it was silly to come, and I think he was right, as per usual. If you *are* irrational, you look better for it. And"—Paola gestured with five perfect, polished nails—"I wouldn't mind trading sanity for the artistic benefits. I've been looking at them, but I don't quite believe it yet. I came here, trembling with fear, expecting you to have cut off an ear like poor van Gogh, but instead, something amazing has happened."

Torey agreed. "I know what you mean. I keep waiting and pinching myself to see if I dreamed the past few weeks. Two years of drought, and now a flood!"

Paola went over ostensibly to examine a small canvas of Peppina sitting at a table and laughing, but she assessed Torey as well. It was her old friend, slender and pretty once again. She looked relaxed, with new, unknown lights in her eyes and a timbre to her voice hinting at new depths.

Torey tried to apologize again for the unnecessary trip but she was hushed immediately. "It's well worth it to know you are well and happy and to see this astounding work," Paola insisted. "You're not your 'old self' as we hoped; you actually seem better than ever, more beautiful, more productive, more . . . everything."

There was a long pause and Paola narrowed her eyes. Torey refused to submit to an inquisition.

"Come on," Paola begged after there was no response. "The reason? Don't stand there and play coy with me. We've been too close for too many years. We can read each other's messages, even the ones written in invisible ink."

"It's Sicily," said Torey lightly. "You and Roberto were wrong. It's given me all the inspiration an artist could want."

"Well, you got more than your share. I imagine you are ready to leave and relax a little?"

"I'm not finished here. There are still a few matters I need to tie up."

Paola smiled very slightly. "But I showed your sketches to Viviano, and he wanted a showing before too long—if the paintings matched the promise the drawings showed. I think those were his words. When can you be packed and ready?"

"I don't know," Torey said. "A day or two. As I said, there are things I have to—"

"Scarpi?" Paola beamed. "I met him very briefly this morning when we arrived. He was just leaving, or so it seemed to me."

"Stop that! There are some things I don't want to discuss at length, even with you."

"Discuss them briefly then," suggested Paola.

"I can't make you understand. I hardly understand it myself. He's vital and attractive, as I'm sure you noticed, and somewhat volatile. He's a man totally committed to his son and his work and more things than I've been able to discover in a short time."

"Significantly, you forgot to mention a woman."

"There seems to be no 'significantly' in that area, Paola. We are not lovers, if you're asking, and it seems clear that even if we were, it would be a temporary, pleasant relationship, nothing more. I want to drop this subject, can we?"

"Let's walk and have lunch, just the two of us," Paola said, too quickly and too obligingly. "I'm so hungry I could eat straw if it had a nice sauce on it."

The atmosphere of fun and good humor was

restored almost immediately. Over a bottle of white wine, they fell easily into the familiar rhythm of long friendship. Paola picked over all the newest scandals in Rome and told Torey about the Fiat case. There was between them the affinity that allowed one to start a sentence and the other to complete it.

Before they left the restaurant, Paola took Torey's hand and gave it a squeeze. "I'm really glad we did come. I was being tormented in Rome with thoughts of you alone and depressed. I wanted to see you before Peppina ever called."

"I'm glad you both came," Torey said simply. "I needed you here to tell me that, if nothing else. You and Roberto were there through some very rough times; it's only fair you share the better days, too."

"Speaking of sharing, there's a very tiny bit of news left to share," Paola whispered, and patted her flat stomach in a smug way.

Torey shrieked in surprised delight. "Oh, when? Paola, I'm so thrilled for you both."

"Roberto is thrilled enough for everyone in Italy, *cara*. Last week he bought an antique cradle in the Thieves' Market, two soccer balls and a doll that can dance the tarantella, I swear. And the baby is not due for months!"

"Christmas! It will be the best present you ever had and the one you've wanted the most." Torey couldn't have been happier, but an old wound was beginning to throb. Paola was only four months older than Torey and they had once agreed that babies, if they came, should arrive before they were thirty-five. There were eight years left, but the years went fast.

"Torey, don't hide what you're thinking. Just this second, you went away from me, you put up the veil. I hate that."

She admitted her pangs of jealousy and Paola dismissed the notion.

"You *will* have your own, I feel sure. And, listen, it's more and more fashionable to get a late start. That is, fashionable everywhere but in wretched places like Sicily, where children appear to have children."

They walked through the city. Palermo seemed so natural and vital to Torey now, in spite of every glaring fault. She hardly noticed the noise and smell that had driven her wild at first. Most of the time was spent discussing the newest Vizzini.

Paola insisted the baby would be a boy and be born with a legal argument on his lips and a very small leather briefcase under one arm. Roberto, always logical and objective, was buying soccer balls and dolls with complete neutrality; he was completely satisfied that any child of his would have his talent, charm and intelligence. He had even suggested Peppina might be persuaded to come back to help Paola after the baby was born.

"I'm really hoping it's a girl," admitted Torey. "I want to see the new Vizzini carry on the tradition of strong, ambitious women."

"Watch it! Stop talking *pro femminista* around here," giggled Paola. "Sicily is absolutely a bastion of male supremacy, or hadn't you noticed? When I think Roberto is being hopelessly medieval in his thinking, I just remember his Sicilian counterparts."

Torey disagreed. "Peppina is one of the ablest,

frankest women I've ever met. Betta has a little of that fire, and I don't think she'll be content with life's scraps or slaving for someone else."

"Perhaps not, Torey, but you don't really know how things are in Italy. Women here have always had strength because they let men think they are kings and then they rule the king."

"I'm not that good an actress." Torey suppressed a shudder. "I let my father rule me, and then Jon led me around. I had no control over my life." And could she be ruled now, or was she stronger?

"You ninny, I'm not talking about acting. You find a man you love, adore and respect—like Roberto— and you let him worship you."

Torey laughed. "If women's liberation ever wins a foothold here, they will hang you with a Vizzini scarf for treason."

"Oh, no," said Paola with great confidence. "They would have to fight my brave Roberto first, and if he couldn't talk them out of it, he'd bore them into submission." She checked her watch and gasped. "We have to get back immediately. It's almost four o'clock and Scarpi left word you were to have dinner with him this evening. You'll never be ready!"

"Don't be silly; I'll wear this outfit."

"Oh, no, you won't! Betta's dress is ready and Scarpi told me this was some sort of celebration."

"I'd like to be consulted first, not last," groaned Torey. "Do you see what I mean?" But Paola was clattering over the pavement, trying to flag a taxi.

* * *

By seven that evening, the bedroom resembled a railway station. Betta moved Torey around in a tight circle, checking the dress hem, while Paola ran in and out. The bed was buried in clothes, underwear and shoes.

"It never took me this long to dress for a prom," grumbled Torey, getting impatient. She had to explain the concept of prom to Betta.

"I'll do your hair again in a minute," shouted Paola from the other room.

"If you do anything else to my hair," Torey sighed, "it will fall out in clumps. I feel ridiculous having you two fawn all over me."

But she submitted; it seemed pointless to fight with them when they were so obviously enjoying the whole production. The dress Betta had made was breathtaking and worth a little fuss. The dark green material, silky and clinging, was fashioned into a classically simple dress. The top was only a soft drape of fabric rising from the waist to circle her neck and fall back, leaving arms, shoulders and a stunning amount of back exposed. The cut, close and daring, made a bra totally impossible, and the long, slim skirt, while not tight, moved gracefully and outlined her slim legs when she walked.

Torey and Paola had been most impressed with the sheer, open kaftan, which floated like a gray and silver cloud over the dress. Any movement brought the silver threads into play and cast pinpoints of light around her. Betta had outdone herself.

"Do you know how many millions of lire this would run in a civilized place?" asked Paola, who

153

knew such things. She spent enough on her own wardrobe.

Betta flushed with pleasure, failing at playing sophisticated designer. "Do you really think it's good, signora Vizzini?"

"Now, don't be impertinent or fish for compliments," cautioned Paola. "It is a fabulous, inspired piece of craftsmanship and you know it. I think you and Peppina and I should have a talk about talent and futures when Cinderella leaves for the ball."

Torey thought the comparison very apt. She felt lost in a fairy tale. The mirror reflected someone unconnected with a painter in filthy jeans and bare feet. Paola had done intricate things with various thin braids and brushed out a long red-brown mane in back.

"What? No crown?" Torey said sarcastically.

"I thought we were on a rescue mission, so I didn't pack the diamonds, *cara*. I had also heard this was not a safe place." Paola thrust a pair of kidskin shoes under Torey's nose and waved a narrow silver belt to match. She stepped back to survey the total effect and nodded at Betta for final approval. The two of them stood back and grinned at each other.

By rights, Torey should have felt silly and uncomfortable. This wasn't her usual style, after all. She'd never had the Vizzini love of fashion or the money to support such a passion. Now, seeing herself in Betta's creation, Torey appreciated Paola's taste much more fully. There was an element of herself being expressed through the dress; it flattered her and made her feel more confident and in control.

"I look beautiful," she said aloud, a bit bemused.

"You are beautiful," corrected Paola. "A dress only enhances, at best, and it can't work miracles. I despise women who need constant reassurance, but frankly, I've never seen you look so marvelous. Well, go ahead to Scarpi; you've kept him waiting long enough even by Roman standards. He's down there in his car, smoking himself into a state."

"*I* kept him waiting? Oh, Paola, you really are impossible!" She kissed them both and wondered if Paola was going to issue the fairy godmother's standard warning. She decided the dress might help bolster her spirits if Andrea was going to play out one of his darker, arcane Sicilian scenes.

Half of Peppina's neighbors were casually draped over their balconies and on the stairs to view Betta's dress as she passed. The exaggerated sighs and florid compliments Torey received reminded her that one of the greatest Italian abilities was the gift of turning any small moment into a historical production. She played to the crowd, smiling and chatting, and they enjoyed it as if they had directed a personal triumph.

Andrea got out of the Alfa Romeo and came around to open the door for her. He pointedly ignored the small crowd following her and, reminiscent of a Roman emperor, appraised her carefully. There had been times when his look flustered or irritated her, but this was not one of those times. She had dressed to be admired. The gentle, constant breeze shifted the transparent kaftan slightly, belling it out behind her, and the audience—but not Andrea —sighed in deep appreciation.

Torey half expected one of his slightly acid, witty remarks, but he didn't offer one. He stepped forward to help her and to look hungrily at her. It took a tremendous amount of control but he did not betray his feelings.

Andrea was a proud man without the handicap of self-delusion that pride often brings. Benedetto's blindness was an irony not lost on him; Andrea had chosen a blind child to remind himself constantly of the dark places pride could take a man. He had been nothing and seen worse. Early memories still pained him, but he forced himself to remember and stay aware of what must be done.

He was proud of his brutal honesty, the edge of which Torey had felt. It wounded him as often as it wounded others, but it kept him free of meaningless entanglements, personal and professional, that hampered other men. He had never taken a bribe, cheated a client or promised the impossible. The cost had been high, but he had paid it willingly in the past, proud of his honesty.

Cefalu had tried him, and he had come dangerously close to compromising a principle he had nurtured for thirty-five years. He had been tempted to watch it blow away into the sea over a cliff when Torey had said yes to him. But she didn't know what having him meant. Tonight she was forcing the issue, looking like a goddess, but she must not misunderstand what he could and would offer her.

As they entered the Massimo's tiled dining rooms he said, "The diners are trying to guess which princess you are." Torey rewarded him with a dazzling smile and kept the thought to herself that he looked like a Saturday matinee pirate in a dinner jacket, dashing and bronzed. They drew discreet but constant stares from the other patrons, distracted momentarily from Palermo's best cuisine and most elegant setting. A couple of tired businessmen overheard the word *principessa*, and the rumor quickly spread through the restaurant that Princess di Longhi was dining there that evening.

A liveried waiter bowed excessively low and held the banquette open until Andrea slid in next to her. The waiter hovered there, a moth at the edge of the light from their table, until Andrea said, "Just give us a real Sicilian feast for the princess tonight."

The man shook with real delight and Torey had to stare with a fixed gaze at the flowers to avoid laughing. The waiter jumped away at attention, omitting very little but a military salute. Then she allowed some of the laughter to bubble up in her throat and scolded Andrea.

"No, it wasn't wicked of me," Andrea insisted with a face lit by mischief. "I gave that man the next best thing to immortality. I, and by your presence you, allowed him a touch of greatness, the one experience all Italians agree is the only prize worth having."

"Peppina used that phrase not so long ago," she said, sipping sweet Moscato from a tall crystal goblet. Its warmth crept into her fingers. Andrea was boyish tonight, full of fun, and systematically charming her without effort. "What's it all about?"

"It's a moment that brings out a great quality in us. Any experience can provide the touch of greatness. If one lives long enough, or gathers wealth or power or love or weight, it can be his own greatness. A great stomach signifies a huge appetite for life as well as pasta; it may explain why there are fat, happy people in here."

"Or is it an act of kindness or charity?" Torey asked. "You were the touch of greatness in Peppina's life, she said."

"Ridiculous!" He poured her more wine and winked. "I am not motivated by unselfish reasons."

"Then I don't see how the waiter achieves any greatness serving a Chicago princess. I'm the great one, aren't I?"

Smiling, with eyes openly admiring her, he was most dangerous. Torey could have lost herself in the blue depths of his look. She shifted her eyes to the little fountain in the corner and hoped the candlelight hid more than it revealed.

"Torey, great beauty qualifies under professor Scarpi's theory, but think carefully! The little waiter has his moment just serving you, the most beautiful woman in Sicily, tonight, and he will tell his children about it."

"I feel tongue-tied when you flatter me," she said.

His brilliant smile vanished completely. "I never flatter," he said flatly and earnestly.

"That's what makes you the ideal critic," Torey remarked. "I have been wondering why you didn't say anything about the paintings."

Without hesitation he said, "I never saw modern works with as much force and feeling as you achieved. Maybe—although the style is very different—maybe in some of Renato Guttuso's paintings. . . ."

She was thunderstruck by the comparison. It was

like having her heart opened and all its secrets read. She had made a private cult of the obscure Sicilian painter years ago. His rare showings and few reproductions had inspired her to once consider making this trip with Jon.

The trays of food arrived in time to save her from babbling happily from the effects of the comparison and the wine. There were at least six different strange but appetizing specialties presented ceremonially to them.

"Now, you must eat everything," kidded Andrea, helping her to a taste of each entrée. "For the poor Chinese children's sake!"

We have our private jokes as if we were lovers, she thought. She asked for more wine, thirsting for something she wouldn't define, and ate with an appetite that surprised her.

"If I had been highly critical of the paintings, what would your reaction have been?" he asked.

Torey stopped, a sliver of swordfish poised on her fork, and considered the idea briefly. "I would have been disappointed. You have obvious taste and knowledge in art, and yet, I know how good this work is. I would have listened to your comments, but it wouldn't have changed how I felt about it. All the changes in my art from now on will come from inside me, not some other critic."

He smiled at the fervent tone and the flash in her green eyes. One day she was a frightened kitten and the next an angry tigress. She spoke with the confidence of a great artist, looking like untouchable royalty. It made him wonder what other dimensions she had hidden.

"You're really quite a puzzle to me," he said. "How can you be so sure of your art and unsure of yourself? Change is natural and good when it helps you paint, but change frightened you when it touched you personally. How can I make sense of Victoria Gardner?"

"You can't." Torey laughed. "I haven't been able to, and I spend lots more time at it, I bet."

"Don't bet," he whispered softly, and took her hand across the table.

"When I discover who Victoria Foreman Gardner is, I'll write a book and send you a copy," promised Torey. "I started looking for her when she was a tall, pudgy girl with braces. She did everything she was told with one exception. She went to art school, following an impulse."

Andrea saw a little of the pain hidden under the light facade, and he could only offer her the strength of his hand for support.

"My father wanted me to be a nurse or a teacher or anything that was a *real* profession, as he called it. My mother is weak and silent; she's always done what he wanted and echoed what he said." She paused, debating whether or not to go on. "When I married Jon, I thought I was free and my own person. But I traded my father's control for Jon's. Because I thought Jon was perfect, it was sufficient for a while to do what he told me and to think what he wanted me to think."

"And then?"

"Maybe we should argue politics or discuss Benedetto," Torey said.

"Go on, Torey, please!" The reality of his

hand, warm and strong, gave her a burst of courage.

"When I began to have shows, Jon was going through a bad time. His work wasn't selling and he wasn't dealing with it well. He lashed out at everyone and everything around him. I was powerless to help him or to stop him. There was no way to soften his anger and, later, his resentment. I almost lost Torey Gardner completely."

"You're finding her now," Andrea said. "Do you like her as much as I do?"

"Yes," she said. "I'm beginning to like her quite a bit." She had a tear caught on her eyelashes and he touched one finger to it, lifting it away.

He promptly proposed a toast to George Washington and the Chicago White Sox to cheer her. She toasted Palermo and its soccer team. The waiter hurried over, eager to bring them dessert or brandy, and he looked crushed when Torey said she would have to be taken out on a stretcher if she ate or drank anything else. The air was stuffy and she was growing uncomfortable.

"I am silly with all the wine," she confided to Andrea. "If I faint and rip this dress, Betta will trim me with pinking shears."

"Let's walk then to the hotel, and you can dance out on the balcony until you're sober."

They left the Massimo in a flurry of bowing and scraping by the staff and were relieved by the cool, calm evening outside. Andrea asked if she was chilled, and his voice held a sly note of criticism.

"You don't like the dress, do you?" she asked.

"I always tell the truth when I'm asked," he

warned. "I enjoy seeing you in it, not showing you off, and there's a difference. I'm hopelessly old-fashioned in some ways, I know. You look exquisite tonight, more beautiful and less attainable as a woman."

She was tempted to say that the dress came off, but she bit her lip. He had the ability, it seemed, to release a wildness in her, and it was an exciting but precarious experience. His own easy swing from mood to mood, quick and spontaneous, was infectious. The faster you leave Sicily, she warned herself, the safer you'll be.

"I enjoyed dinner so much I forgot to ask you something very important," Andrea continued. "I had planned a little talk, but perhaps if we dance, I'll find the right words to charm you into doing a favor for me."

"Have you ever heard of a man so charming he could get hair to grow on a bald lady's head?" she asked. When he admitted he hadn't, Torey said he fit that description and it made her suspicious.

He wouldn't reply or give her a hint, but escorted her to the hotel's dance floor silently. The second he put his arm around her and she felt the touch of his hand on her bare back, she knew a moment of panic. She had stopped drinking champagne, but that was not the only wine she was drunk on. Her knees were unsteady and every place their bodies touched became fiery hot. Because of his height, she had to look up to speak to him, and the soft air of his breath caressed her face when he answered her.

His right hand moved lazily, strong fingers stroking her skin as if he were tracing letters on her. If she tried to move away from him, he tightened his grip and pulled her firmly to him. He bent his dark head down and brought his lips against her ear in a gentle kiss.

"I want you to stay a few more days in Sicily," he said. "I'll put you on the plane for Rome myself, but I need a few days of your time. It's important!"

"I can't," she said quietly. "Paola and Roberto and I are leaving tomorrow afternoon. They've made all the arrangements."

He dropped her right hand and touched her lips with his finger. His eyes looked black, not blue, under the shadow of his brow, and she couldn't look away from him.

"Please, hear me out and then decide."

She nodded assent, not trusting herself to speak coherently.

"Let's sit down and talk," he suggested. "It's not easy to be rational and persuasive standing this close to you."

"I can't avoid leaving," Torey said. "I did wait to see you tonight. . . ."

"I'm not asking this just for myself," he said. "I drove back from Carboi yesterday after the school called me about Benedetto. He was very upset and unhappy and I had to send him on to Trapani yesterday morning. I'm going there tomorrow"—he looked at his watch—"actually today, myself."

"It was my visit, wasn't it?" asked Torey miserably. "I can't pretend to understand it all, but somehow I really upset him and he felt I was deserting him."

Andrea slipped his hand under her chin and

forced her to meet his eyes. "It's a serious case of a broken heart for an eight-year-old, but it can be cured relatively easily. It became clear to me that because you are the first woman I've introduced him to in a very long time, and because he has a real affinity for you, he made up a childish but not unreasonable fantasy that you would stay and be his mother. I blame myself for not explaining things more specifically to him."

She wondered if Andrea had any notion of the force of his personality on her. She felt she would be drawn to him anywhere or anytime. "I saw a hunger in him to be loved."

"Yes," Andrea agreed, "and he and I talked about it for a long while. I am very often away from him and for a long time. When I adopted him, I didn't envision what the job of father would entail. Come to Trapani with me and spend a few days. Let him know he can love, even if it's not forever."

"I should know that story by heart," she said. "But, Andrea, he won't speak to me. At least, he wouldn't."

"He wants to see you and he doesn't, all at once. He is beginning to want more from life than he's been given. When I was his age I didn't have much time to sit and think, but he does. Thinking is dangerous sometimes, isn't it?"

He ran his thumb over her silver ring but made no mention of it.

"What if time with me only intensifies these feelings?" she asked. "I don't want him hurt more." *And I don't want to be hurt,* she added mentally. "Sometimes you frighten me, Andrea."

"The boy has to learn that everyone who goes away is not deserting him the way his mother did four years ago. He's blind, Torey, and I don't want him crippled as well. As for us, nothing will happen that is not right, that you don't want. You have my word on that!"

He meant every word; it was written in his face, open and frank. She trusted him, but she dared not trust herself. He had asked her for help, and he was so proud, it must have been difficult. Torey considered what she was committing herself to as he took her hand and buried his lips in her open palm. She felt her last chance at peace and safety slipping away.

"If you want me to beg you, I will—for Benedetto's sake," he whispered.

"No," she said, "don't beg." He had won. "You've been responsible for a lot of the good things that have happened to me. I can't promise I'll do much good, but I'll try."

He hadn't asked her to stay with him for his own sake, and the realization hurt a tiny bit. She wanted to help Benedetto, but she knew she wanted the time with Andrea almost as much.

Chapter Nine

$\mathscr{P}$aola rolled over and grabbed the phone on the third ring. Torey had to repeat herself twice before the sense, or nonsense, of what she was saying penetrated the fog of sleep. Paola shifted the receiver and propped herself up on the pillows, checking the clock. Two in the morning and Torey was packing a suitcase? Roberto slept on, blissfully snoring.

"Torey, we are not leaving until late this afternoon."

"I'm going to Trapani for a few days with Andrea. We are leaving in four hours." She ran down a mental checklist. "Did you bring a swimsuit with you, by any chance? I'll probably need one."

Paola sat bolt upright, fully awake. "You must have had quite an evening. I thought this was to be a tender good-bye with a friend, and now you're running away in four hours. I have a few questions of my own."

Torey described the evening and the discussion of Benedetto briefly. Paola restrained herself, making none of her usual quips or comments, but listened carefully.

"I understand more than you're saying," she exclaimed at the end of Torey's explanation. "I just hope you can deal with your feelings as easily as you think you can deal with the boy. You know what you're doing, I hope, and what you want, but are you ready for this?"

"I'll chance it," Torey said. "I feel like a whole woman again and I have to find out. I can't leave with Benedetto on my conscience. I don't want to run away all the time."

"Good," Paola said. "Good for you, but think first about you and your work and go slowly. You stay and I'll take the paintings back with us and deliver them personally into Viviano's greedy but capable hands. I'll be waiting for you in Rome."

"You said that as if you don't expect me," Torey commented.

An eloquent pause. "Who knows? You are taking a chance, thinking you can handle Andrea Scarpi without falling head over heels, but do what you must! I'm trying to tell you to be careful, Torey."

"I'm not going to get derailed," she said with feeling. "I am just a little sidetracked, perhaps."

Paola promised she would handle everything and inform Peppina that Torey would be back later in the week to say good-bye. Torey packed quickly, checking in every room, and left the dress where Paola couldn't fail to see it. The paintings were a tangible reminder of what she had accomplished the last few weeks and of how abruptly her life had changed. Getting back into life, she mused, was a lot like Paola's having a baby. It would take a long time developing in secret, with an element of mystery and, unfortunately, an element of risk attached. *Whatever it takes,* she vowed, *I'm not running from it again.* One minute she was deliriously happy and the next unsure of everything. But she would risk being foolish or getting into deep waters, and that was a start.

"I'm really sorry." Torey yawned. "I must have dozed off crossing the Jato. You were pointing out all the dam's features, and that's the last thing I remember. Where are we now?"

The car shot around another hairpin turn and accelerated up a long, smooth rise. To her right, the sun flashed off the sea and burned away the last of the gray morning mists. June could be sultry, but out here the air was fresh and had a bracing effect on her. Torey rolled down the window and tried to wake up in the cool breeze.

Andrea's brown hands rested lightly on the wheel, correcting the steering with minute, sure movements. "We're about two kilometers past Trappeto. I thought we might stop in Castellammare for fuel, and then we'll be just an hour away from Trapani."

The unmistakable scent of eucalyptus from a

roadside grove rushed through the car. It seemed they were hundreds of miles from Palermo's teeming streets, but Torey had looked at the map and Trapani was only three hours from the capital. The sky was a brilliant, unstreaked plane of blue from horizon to horizon, without clouds or the smoke of the city. They shot past orchards of lemon and orange, which gave the air a faint citrus taste.

The kilometer markers were flashing by in rapid succession, dizzying her. A gap in the low hills and rocks revealed the ocean stretching out forever for one brief moment, and then it vanished. Torey had a sudden vision of Lake Michigan from the Outer Drive and put her hand up to her eyes to erase the thought as well as the image. The Alfa negotiated the next curve easily, but a sense of dread had been sparked in her.

"Could you slow down a bit," she asked, "and let me . . . enjoy the view?"

Andrea glanced down at the speedometer. He was below the speed limit, but he eased off the accelerator and geared the car down. The powerful engine hummed in a lower key.

It didn't help. The fear inside her began to spread, tightening her stomach and making her palms slippery with sweat. "Slow down," she repeated with a rising note of panic in her voice.

When he glanced over, puzzled, he saw the glassy look in her eyes, and her hands, so tightly curled the nails were digging into flesh. "I'm a good driver, Vittoria," he said matter-of-factly, "and not just by Italian standards. Are you frightened?"

Her reply was silenced by a lump in her throat.

"You're thinking about something else, aren't you, and not my driving? If I seem reckless to you, I will let you drive to Trapani after we stop to stretch our legs. Will that satisfy you?" The scarred eyebrow went up. He reminded himself that an oyster produces a pearl only after it is irritated by a foreign object. "Or can't you drive?"

"Damn you," Torey snapped. "I haven't driven a car in two years—since Jon's accident. Will you slow down?" She leaned toward him, prepared to turn the key off in the ignition, but he had anticipated her and caught her wrist in his viselike grip. He didn't take his eyes off the road, nor would he release her hand.

"You want to provoke me, I think," he said quietly. "Which of us is the most unreasonable?"

"You," she said with all the venom she could muster. "You cajole me into this trip by appealing to my sense of guilt and claim we put all our differences behind us, like our unpleasant scene at Cefalu. Now, it looks like an encore performance."

The tiny village of Castellammare was around the next hill. Andrea drove into the gas station, parked and, in the universal manner of men, got out to talk with the attendant.

"Let's go across the road and get something to eat while he makes a few adjustments," he invited her. "It's better than sulking in the car."

She seethed inwardly but blamed no one but herself. This was the way things had to be with Andrea, and she had made the decision to come, no one else. She poured them each a cup of thick, foamy cappuccino and spread two rolls with fresh butter, acting the gracious lady.

"Thank you," Andrea said with some surprise. "It's so easy to forget how nice a woman's company can be. I have spent too much time without the niceties, I think."

The owners of the café, a thin man with a pronounced limp and his stately Amazon of a wife, knew Andrea well. They brought over more rolls and a small copper pot with trailing jasmine to the table. The man bowed formally over Torey's hand and chatted briefly with Andrea in very thick dialect.

"What was that all about?" she asked after the owner left. "I heard something about congratulations, but the rest was unintelligible."

"He wished us a long and happy life together and many heirs." He smiled when she looked uncomfortable.

"Well, I hope you told him we weren't married!"

"You constantly forget where you are, Vittoria. In Chicago, or perhaps in Rome, a man can travel freely with a lady who is not his wife. In Sicily, the possibility would not be mentioned; it would be a grave insult to your reputation. Before you object too strongly, let me say again—things are as they are. Men here are still concerned with honor, family and pride. We are hopelessly behind the rest of the world in abandoning those ideals."

"Then the man doesn't think we are married! He's just acting the right way?"

"What he thinks is immaterial and private. He acts correctly and assumes we will return the favor."

"And the next time you stop here and there's

another Mrs. Scarpi with you?" The thought that she might not be the first or last woman to enjoy coffee here was irritating.

"My friend is a gentleman. He'd never mention it."

"To pretend well is the highest ideal?" Torey wanted to see him on the defensive and off-balance just once.

Andrea didn't bristle at all. "No, the highest ideal is to do things correctly, being what you are. I see, Vittoria, that many things I do and say strike you as very wrong, but believe me, I am trying to do things well." He broke off a short sprig of jasmine and ran it lightly over her hand. "Sometimes I am too direct, but we don't have much time."

She was not going to be fooled by the tender gesture or the soft look he gave her. Torey knew how stubborn and cruel he could be, as when he was driving into town. This look of his, making electricity dance along her arms, was equally a prelude to an embrace or a battle. She glanced at her watch, misunderstanding his remark. "It's not even ten o'clock yet. You said Trapani was only an hour from here."

"Not *that* time," he said cryptically. "The mechanic has to adjust the carburetor; we have time to finish our coffee." When Torey refused to rise to his bait, Andrea plunged in after her. "I want to talk to you, Torey, without you flying into a rage or crying. I assure you, I am not trying to provoke you. I'm hoping to be very civilized. After all, the debate is an ancient tradition here."

She nodded, thinking she had accurately predicted this storm. "I'm not very good at handling Sicilian explosions of emotion. I like to discuss things quietly."

"But you got angry when I asked you if you were afraid of a reality or a memory. Do you feel threatened or unfaithful when I bring your husband to mind?"

Her back stiffened slightly at the reference to Jon and she didn't answer him.

He would not allow himself to be moved only by pity for her and continued, "You see, you are doing it this very minute. You react so badly, it seems unnatural to me. Especially when I asked you to come with me to help Benedetto understand that people come and go in life, how it must be expected and dealt with honestly. All the while, there is the impenetrable wall of your past." He passed one hand roughly through his thick black hair, and the beautiful liquid fluidity of his speech seemed harsh and forced. "Benedetto is consumed by hatred of a woman he can't remember and it makes him fearful of loving again. And you, *cara?*"

Torey heard every word as if she sat at the bottom of a well, but she heard them. Andrea was not cool and detached; his manner and the tension in his voice told her he truly cared about her.

"The past is still with me," she said, "but the horror of it is almost gone. I know I wasn't responsible for Jon's death, but there are times when anger and guilt overtake me, stopping me from going on with my life. I'm changing, Andrea, and it's painful.

I guess it's natural to want to retreat when I'm fearful."

She poured out some of her deepest fears and lingering doubts without censoring each thought and every word. It rolled in a huge tidal wave to Andrea, who let her words break harmlessly against him and roll away into quieter waters. He saw relief fill her and he marveled at the hidden strength she called on. It had been worth any risk to see her emerge from darkness and look around at her new world.

"You must share some of these ideas with Benedetto," he said softly, "if you can. He can't go on hating a stranger and afraid of a future. My memories and I have an uneasy peace, at best."

"I feel," Torey sighed, noting her trembling hands, "as if I'd run here from Palermo."

"You've come pretty far, Vittoria, since we first met. The car must be ready, if you are."

He started to get up but she put a light, restraining hand on his arm. "Andrea, I've been difficult and wrong in things I've said to you. Why are you going to all this trouble for me?"

His strong fingers gripped hers tightly. "We have shared a lot of sweetness, too. We'll have the next few days to learn more about each other without bitterness between us."

They crossed the road, hand in hand, and waved at the cafe's owners. Andrea reached into his pocket and pulled out the key ring.

"The speed limit is 140 kilometers per hour. For you, 90 miles an hour." And he tossed her the keys. "I didn't get much sleep either last night. I was out drinking and dancing with an absolutely gorgeous woman."

Torey slid in behind the wheel and started the powerful engine up without a second thought. The road wound and dipped ahead and the wind filled her ears with a mad rush. Andrea did not sleep, preferring to sing her all his favorite arias and teasing her into adding her terrible, tone-deaf contributions to familiar choruses. Her hair flew around her face in wild, whipping snakes of red and bronze. He noticed she drove fast and expertly and, after a while, with the kind of pleasure he enjoyed in controlling speed and power.

They reached Trapani within the hour. After the buildup from Andrea and Benedetto, Torey was disappointed by her first view of "The City of the Four Winds." It was small but very definitely a city, dreary and modern, while she had expected a quaint, pretty fishing village. Andrea stopped in the middle of a song and urged her to drive through the tall buildings.

"It looks as though if I drive out much farther, we'll be swimming in the sea," Torey insisted.

"Right. We're on the peninsula that goes into the Tyrrhenian Sea, but keep going down there." He pointed to the narrowing strip of land.

The city fell behind them and the car moved slowly, following the curved finger of land tickling the waters beyond. There were very few houses, and these were all dazzling white cubes set precariously onto the edge of the land. Some looked as if they would slip down the sloping sands any minute. There was a timeless, lost quality to this place. A few children waved to them, wading in shallow tide pools.

"This is old Trapani," announced Andrea, "and that, all alone, is my house. Go very slowly or we'll be able to net our lunch from the car windows." He smiled with undisguised delight to be here.

Benedetto and a portly woman Torey guessed was Teresa came out of the front door. The house appeared to be exactly like the others they had passed, squat and freshly whitened and small. A riot of small flowers grew in the narrow roadway, and every window had a jungle of plants decorating it.

Andrea jumped out of the car and swung a squealing Benedetto high over his head. They covered each other with kisses, laughing and totally oblivious to anyone else. Teresa stood primly posed to one side, with her hands neatly clasped together. Torey drank in the scene, enjoying their joy but feeling awkward. Behind her, she could still glimpse the new city's tall towers and the spires of churches and the rigging of ships in the old harbor. It was a chance to stand in yesterday and look at modern times from far away.

Andrea put Benedetto down and called to her. She went into the yard, almost shy, terribly unsure of her reception. Benedetto heard the crunch of gravel and shells under her shoes and moved toward her.

"It's so good to be here with you," she said. "Oh, Benedetto, forgive me for making you unhappy." She knelt down so she could see his face. "And I wore the carnation perfume for you."

He ran to the sound of her voice, throwing himself into her open arms. Benedetto nuzzled her neck like a puppy, sniffing the spicy scent for reassurance. Then he kissed her on both cheeks in a proper greeting.

"When Papa told me you would come, I told him I didn't want to see you ever again. He just laughed and made a joke I didn't understand, but I did want you to come. I did, Torey!"

She stood up and held on to the boy tightly. "I understand and so I came. We'll have some time to spend any way we want. And we won't waste it standing around when we could be swimming or eating! Help me with my luggage and we'll get busy."

Andrea introduced her to Teresa as they started into the house. Torey wondered if the woman was a mute; she said nothing, merely nodding curtly and then stalking into the house.

"Leave the suitcase," Andrea said at the door. "We can unpack later, but first we'll eat."

Teresa offered them a cold plate of fresh fruit and fat, pink shrimp with an icy smooth wine to accompany it. Benedetto drank a glass of wine mixed with water and offered the first toast.

"To Trapani, the place I love best, and the people I love best with me."

Torey was touched by her inclusion, but it was worrisome, too. Leaving here was not going to be easier when the boy seemed more attached to her every time they were together. All during the lunch, he found excuses to touch her hand or face. Worst of all, he touched her heart, and it was not going to be an easy departure for her. After Benedetto finished, Andrea excused him to wash up and change for a swim. Torey watched the boy leave, totally confident and at ease in these familiar surroundings.

"You designed the house for him, didn't you?" She looked around the great open room they were in. Everything had a sense of airiness and smoothness, without corners or edges. Furniture stood pressed near the rough walls so there were no hazards to trip a blind child. The great room was living and dining area all in one, with a fine, modern kitchen at one end. The few doorways were wide and arched.

Andrea said, "He must have one place in the world that is his, totally safe and free. I know he will cope with the world and its dangers, but not here. This is his home."

The house's small exterior was deceiving. Inside it was open and spacious, with unpolished quarry tile floors. The couches and chairs were modern but comfortable. Color was everywhere and bright, pleasing her eye, but rough textures were used to delight the boy's sense of touch. She had wondered if the house had electricity and running water and felt foolish confronted by modern appliances next to racks of black, heavy pots and antique stoneware dishes.

"I'm proud of the house, in case you couldn't tell," he said, following her gaze. "I'll show off the rest and then let's swim."

"I still don't have a suit," Torey admitted, "because there wasn't time to buy one."

Andrea looked around for the silent Teresa. "Her daughter, Gina, often visits here, and sometimes she swims with Benedetto. I'm sure there's a suit around somewhere. Go ahead and look while I find Teresa."

Torey walked down the hallway slowly, looking at the paintings, all originals and signed by Italians, many of whom she didn't know. Niches were recessed smoothly into the wall itself, and Andrea had small statues at a height she could view but which were clearly meant for Benedetto's touch. The first room off the hall was Benedetto's room and she peeked in.

The boy was lying on the floor, propped on one side and reading a large Braille edition of a book before him. He was intent, lost in his story. The shelves around the room were neatly organized with cars and trucks, planes and shells in row after row. His special books had a case near a desk, and only the absence of any desk lamp indicated it was the room of an extraordinary child. Textures ran from the plush carpet to the latticed walls. Sage, mint and rosemary bloomed in Benedetto's window box, gratifying his sense of smell.

It convinced her more firmly than ever that Andrea was an unusual man. He seemed so callous at times and yet had expended a gargantuan effort to provide the boy with an oasis from the world's indifference.

Her room, with her suitcase on the bed, was sparsely furnished with old carved furniture and a wildly colored quilt. The windows, with white louvered shutters, overlooked the tiny strip of road and across the sea beyond. It might have been a state-room on a boat, not a room. There were no other houses in sight, only the blaze of light on water.

Andrea's bedroom was very large and overlooked the beach of brown, sloping sand. She stopped at the doorway and wondered at the absence of another door. It was a man's room, without any feminine hand to soften its look. The huge bed had a massive old headboard with rough carvings she couldn't see clearly. It was austere and plain, with a chest of drawers and a desk for Andrea's work. The only painting on the wall made her gasp when she realized it was, indeed, a Guttuso original of an eruption of Mt. Etna.

"You could walk in and get a better look," suggested Andrea from behind her. He handed her a tank suit of the new Olympic variety. She went in and looked over the beautiful watercolor carefully. Finally, she turned and waved the swimsuit like a child's flag.

"Gina must be ten years old, Andrea. If I wear this, large portions of me will be left out."

"Gina is sixteen and very mature," he said. "Have faith in modern materials; this will stretch to any limit." Taking aim, he tossed the suit on her bed. "And remember, my beach is very private. The boulders at both ends keep Benedetto in boundaries and keep wandering tourists out. Now, change before he has apoplexy from waiting so long for his swim!"

She undressed, doubtful that a shiny piece of blue elastic this size would fit as anything other than a headband. But the sea looked calm and inviting.

Andrea's claims for the marvels of modern technology seemed to be true; the suit slid on easily, but she couldn't resist a puckish smile when she looked in the mirror. If Betta's dress worn in public had bothered him, she wondered what his reaction to the suit would be. Torey had never been particularly modest, and after years of drawing models and being drawn, she never gave nudity much thought. She might as well swim without it as wear it, she decided. She threw her old robe around her and grabbed up extra towels.

Benedetto and Andrea were busy, already in the water. Benedetto was swimming out to Andrea's instructions and then, with a flip turn, heading confidently back into the shallows. The boy swam well, reminding her of his boasts of Andrea's medals. It was clear that long hours of coaching had been spent. She left her robe and towels on the coarse sand and waded into the sea slowly. It was tepid and she could see all the way to the bottom, except when a small wave hurried by her to disappear into the brown beach. Torey dove in cleanly and swam far out until her arms began to ache with the unaccustomed exercise, then she swam smoothly back to where they were playing.

"I don't advise going too far out," Andrea cautioned her. "The beach drops off very sharply, and there are tricky crosscurrents and undertows."

He stood in waist-deep water with small droplets clinging like quicksilver to his tanned shoulders and back. He was leaner but more well muscled than she had suspected, as if he labored hard for a living, and his broad, knotted shoulders tapered dramatically to a narrow waist and flat stomach. She had drawn young male models with similar physiques, but it had been impersonal then, concentrated on a shadow or a line and only professionally interesting. Torey wanted to reach out and touch him, to feel the texture of smooth skin with the hardness of muscle underneath. Her swim alone didn't account for the shallowness of her breathing and the sharp, sudden stricture in her chest.

"I'm a strong swimmer," she said, "but I don't have any medals to prove it."

He gave her a wry smile and pointed out that on her suit there was no place to pin a medal without serious damage to the wearer.

"You insisted," she reminded him. "Sicilian morals or not, it's this blue rubber band or nothing."

"I would opt for nothing then, Vittoria," he said, "but even if Benedetto wouldn't be corrupted, Teresa is very old-fashioned."

The blatant remark excited her because it matched her own tension at seeing him, and she couldn't think of a clever thing to say. Benedetto insisted she watch him swim the backstroke and the crawl and the butterfly, and she was grateful to have something to do other than stand and stare at Andrea.

She and the boy spent the better part of two hours playing. He loved to show off his prowess and reveled in her attention and compliments. Andrea took the chance to swim alone and Torey saw him move cleanly and swiftly through the sea with a graceful, unhurried stroke. While Andrea rested on the beach, she and Benedetto mimicked the dolphins, diving straight down and deep, then surfacing in a great fountain of foam.

"I think you should let Torey rest awhile, Benedetto," Andrea called. "We drove here without much sleep, and old people tire easily, you know. Play close in and we can swim again in a while."

She put the rolled towel under her head for a pillow and relaxed. "I'm grateful you dragged me away. I'm tired from playing with him, with all that boundless energy."

"Actually, I was getting a little jealous of his monopoly on your company." He laughed.

When she closed her eyes against the sun's brilliance, the blaze of red she saw reminded her of Cefalu and she opened them quickly. Andrea sat near her, keeping Benedetto in sight. She remembered the touch of Andrea's mouth on hers that day, the heat of his breath against her throat. *Stop it,* she told herself firmly, *before you spoil the day and make yourself miserable.* She fell asleep immediately, a sweet, deep nap.

She woke lying in shade and, looking up, saw a large green canvas umbrella had been propped over her. Andrea was stretched out next to her, but Benedetto had disappeared.

"Why didn't you wake me up?" she said. "I'm a great guest, aren't I?"

"I promised Benedetto you would hunt shells with him in the morning but you needed to sleep. You were smiling while you slept; are you happy here?"

"I feel good for no particular reason, so I guess so. This seems to be an easy place to feel happy."

"You looked like a little pagan statue of the Erican Venus when you were sleeping. I used the time to study you." He bent over and kissed her mouth lightly, pressing her back on the towel and kissing her again, increasing the pressure and the demand on her to respond.

"I really can't be patient much longer, Torey," he whispered. "I want you badly. Don't make me wait."

"Here, in broad daylight? With Teresa and Benedetto around?" Torey wondered if he was teasing her cruelly.

Andrea hooked his thumbs under the suit's straps and drew them slowly down over her shoulders. "Benedetto fell sound asleep a few minutes ago in his room. Teresa is gone for today." He kissed the hollow of her throat and said, "I don't have to wait for darkness on my own beach." His fingers grazed her hardened nipples, making her ache and move under his touch.

The first fluttering response to him surged into a distinct pulse of pleasure through her body. Torey put her arms around him, caressing the back of his tanned, muscled neck, and kissed him eagerly, welcoming the leisurely exploration of his tongue and the hard pressure of his teeth. Her back arched to raise her sensitive breasts against the firmness of his chest.

The thin suit peeled away easily under his fingers and he slowly exposed her fully to his touch and his kiss. His mouth followed wherever his fingers wandered, lingering to enjoy the curve of her waist and trailing with agonizing slowness across her stomach.

He traced small, stroking patterns along her hips and found the silken, heated skin of her thighs taut with excitement. The suit slipped down her legs and he kissed the hollows behind her knees, stroking the soft roundness of her calves. No one, she realized, her pulse quickening, had touched her this way, this completely.

She watched him slip off his own trunks and heard herself moan involuntarily. He was more powerful and beautiful in his arousal than she could have dreamed; her fingers reached out, longing to touch him. She wanted him to cover her nakedness with his own flesh, but he stretched out on his side next to her and would not be hurried.

Andrea's lips moved lightly, barely brushing her skin, first tasting and then feasting on her. The tip of his tongue circled her breast and teased gently at the nipple until his teeth captured his prize and he heard her gasp of pleasure. An exploring hand swept possessively down her body and parted her thighs, finding the moist warmth of desire. She shuddered and moved under the slow probe of his fingers, aware that he was deliberate and controlled while she grew more helpless with delight.

Torey turned toward him, fusing her body to the long, hard length of him, and tried somehow to express the sweet, primitive excitement she felt. There were no words she knew that would be adequate; she pleaded with her eyes, coaxing him with her own light touches and eager lips.

"Yes," he whispered, understanding. His breath burned her ear and cheek and throat while his hands pulled her pliant hips closer. He moved against her slowly, teasingly, his hard flesh demanding a response and expertly commanding it. He pressed her back down and felt her open to him, like a flower unfolding.

"So beautiful. You are almost too beautiful." He groaned. Even now, as her body rose to accept him and hold him, he forced himself to take her slowly, prolonging the joy of their union and pleasing her first.

She clung to him, clutching at his back, and was only conscious of an endless, growing urgency within her. A hundred separate throbbings in her blended and merged into a fullness of sensation she didn't recognize. Her own strange frenzy and the hoarse cries she dimly heard were almost frightening. Her body twisted and writhed in new ways, responding to the agonizingly slow, steady movements he made above her. Her fingers found his muscled buttocks and raked along his thighs.

"Let it happen," he ordered hoarsely. "Torey, let it happen." He matched his demand with sure, almost savage motion to force her immediate and complete surrender.

She pressed her face deep in the joining of his neck and shoulder and cried out. She was sure she had broken free of her body and floated somewhere else, far away, knowing nothing but the wonderful release he had given her. It thrilled her to hear his echo of fulfillment and to know she had returned a precious gift.

He held her tightly against himself, unwilling to end the ultimate moment of closeness. "You're not sorry, are you, *bella?*"

"No, no," she insisted quickly, seeing real concern in his eyes. "I would never regret anything so wonderful. You are tender and considerate and overwhelming. I felt caught up in an earthquake." As soon as she said the word, Torey recalled Peppina's reference to the *terremoto* and there was no need to ask Andrea; she understood. It was the counterpart to "the thunderbolt"—a passion that built slowly inside and lay hidden under a rocky exterior, growing stronger the longer it was suppressed. Once the earthquake began, there was no control, only a surrender to a force far beyond her experience.

He held her next to him for a long time, silently. The shadows on the beach were lengthened into rich purple velvets, dark blues moving into black. The sun set in clouds of pink and peach, glowing on their skin. Torey brushed sand from his arms and felt the cool touch of evening on her damp body. Andrea took her robe and covered her at the sound of the door opening.

"Papa? Torey?" Benedetto came toward them, his hair still rumpled from sleep. "I can't find a thing to eat, Papa, and I'm really starving!"

"So was I," Andrea whispered to Torey as he helped her into her robe. "But my appetites are not as easily satisfied as his." To the boy he called, "Didn't Teresa leave us anything?"

"No," whined Benedetto. "She must have been mad at us. Is it dark yet?"

Torey drew him down next to her, asked him if he remembered colors and described the sky, now salmon and blood-red. He knew only the difference between the sun's light and the great, cold darkness of night and said he pretended colors, thinking of them as tastes for the eyes.

"Please, feed this boy," laughed Torey. "All he thinks about is filling his stomach. He must be growing an inch a day!"

Andrea hugged the boy and smoothed down a wild cockscomb of hair. "Now, Vittoria, you know all the dark secrets of the Scarpi. We can enjoy life only on a full stomach. While you change, I'll cook us a treat with Benedetto as assistant."

"Cuscusu," shrieked Benedetto in a wail that startled a passing bird.

"That's an Arabic dish," Torey said. "Here, in Sicily?"

"Look." Benedetto gestured across the ocean in the approximate direction. "Africa's only eighty-five miles away from us, and sometimes, when the wind is right, you can smell the jungles or find things washed up on our beach."

"You've spoiled my surprise," said Andrea, running his knuckles over Benedetto's head. "I am an unbeatable chef when it comes to *cuscusu.* You can ask anyone, as long as it is my favorite, unbiased customer," he added, pointing at the boy.

"World class swimmer, gourmet chef," Torey kidded. "Is there no end to your talents?"

"I like to think my finest qualities," he said, looking across Benedetto at her, "are not widely known." He kissed her at the corner of her mouth and touched her face.

"Are you kissing?" moaned Benedetto. "Why did

we stop walking? Papa, we'll never eat supper at this rate."

"My apologies," Andrea said, "and you're absolutely right, *caro*. The meal usually comes before the dessert. I'm just happy Torey is here with us."

"Me, too," said Benedetto, "but I'm still hungry."

"I can sympathize." But Andrea's look was of another hunger. "And tonight, let's only speak English at the table. Torey can untangle our metaphors before we trip on them."

The evening was one of those rare times that, even as it happened, Torey knew she would hold on to as a good memory forever. She felt certain that years later she would accurately recall the spice-rich scent of Andrea's dinner cooking while the chef sang loudly to it, "encouraging it," he insisted. Her inner eye would recreate fine details long after: the ivory light on Benedetto's small face, the threads of rough linen under her fingertips, and the meal held together with a ribbon of laughter woven through the night.

Best of all, she treasured and stored a look of simple, unguarded peace on Andrea's face. He had tried, for the third time, to get her to repeat a proverb in the harsh, guttural dialect. He and Benedetto struggled unsuccessfully not to laugh at her but ended holding each other in helpless mirth at her imitation of their growls and hisses. Torey would keep his face, like a painting, in her mind; the look of joy and contentment had softened the angular lines of his handsome face and made the piercing blue eyes light and free of wariness. The hard, firm line of his mouth was relaxed and gentled. It summed up for her something she wanted desperately for herself, a feeling she had endlessly and almost hopelessly pursued, until this place and this evening.

Chapter Ten

Torey and Benedetto carefully picked their way among the towering black rocks, wading through small, warm pools of tidewater, bending and sifting in the sea lettuce and debris for shells. The wind came across the beach with a whisper from Africa, heavy with the scent of black soil and lush jungles. When Torey stood up from time to time and looked out at the Tyrrhenian, the horizon was smudged with a ship, far off and part of another, more hurried, world.

"Don't you think we should leave a shell or two on the beach?" she asked the boy, putting down the box she was carrying filled with the collected treasures. "We could set up a small stand at the wharf and sell these to tourists right now."

He came over and ran his sensitive, questing fingers through their stock, agreeing reluctantly that they had enough. He pulled out one perfect conch with seven crown points and traced it over with care.

"This one is for you, Torey, to keep. You call Neptune with this shell."

She pushed russet hair futilely behind her ears, only to have the wind spread it playfully across her face. "Now, why would I bother the old god? He's been out of the business of helping mortals for a long time; I heard he retired hundreds and hundreds of years ago."

"Papa doesn't think so. Sometimes when we talk, he tells me all about the ancient gods worshipped here. He said he thinks they're still around, inside the rocks and trees, in the earth and under the sea, just waiting. They can't leave us, so they've all gone to sleep and are resting until we want them again—if we ever do."

Was it only the breeze that made her shudder? She wrapped the too-big sweater Andrea had lent her tighter and hugged her arms around herself. It was true; the pagan past of Sicily lay just under the sea's surface and lurked in the massive rocks around them. The fleeting peace of yesterday was the illusion. The hard reality, the wildness of this place, had endured through centuries, shaping the people as it tortured their lives.

"You had better not let Sister Veronica or Angela hear you talk like that, little barbarian," she said.

Benedetto chuckled, "I am a good Catholic and a very good Sicilian. I can keep secrets and do the right things with no trouble at all."

"Why are we going to the harbor this morning?" Torey asked, eager to change the subject. "Your Papa was vague at breakfast this morning about our plans."

"It's *La Mattanza* all this week and you will get to see it," explained Benedetto. "You can't imagine how exciting the tuna catch is until you have been there. Last year was the first time Papa would take me, and there was so much noise I couldn't get answers to all my questions. This time, you'll be there and you can paint me my word picture of the fishing."

"Well, I'm not a big fan when it comes to hunting or fishing, *caro*," she said quietly. "I can't imagine why people want to stand on boats for hours watching other people haul in fish."

"But we must go!" begged Benedetto. "It's a very old and very special festival for Trapani when the tuna schools come by. Please!"

Soon, she thought, she would be back in Rome with Paola, planning a nursery or consulting with Viviano, and this would be a dream she'd had. At least it was a good dream for a change. She reached over and stroked his cheek with the back of her hand. "Of course, we'll go. I will want to paint hundreds of pictures of Trapani, you and the tuna fishers when I get back to Rome."

He pushed her hand away angrily and turned his face to the sea. His voice was strident but there was a note of fear, as well. "You mustn't go away. You could stay here with us, with me, forever. I don't want you to leave, no matter what Papa says."

Links of steel constricted around her heart and

slowed the beating to a painful thud. "What did Papa tell you, Benedetto? That I would have to go to work and be with my friends soon? It's true. Did he say I was only visiting for a few days? I must leave; there's so much for me to do."

"There's so much to do here. I would be a good boy and help you cook and help you paint . . ." Here he lost his fight to be manly and began to cry. The tears hung on his cheeks until she brushed them away with cold fingers. The boy crumpled sideways and fell into her arms, sobbing with deep, hiccoughing gasps. All he could manage to say was "No . . . no" in a desolate little voice.

"Benedetto," she whispered, pushing back the fine sable hair and rocking him gently, "you must listen to me. I'll share a secret with you, a very grown-up secret, and then you'll understand. Don't cry, baby, or you'll make me cry too."

The milky eyes stared up at her and the steel chain binding her heart cut it nearly in two. The boy's lips quivered but he quieted.

"I love it here with you . . . and Papa," she said. "I've been so happy I came, but . . ." She faltered, then forced herself on. "I have my work, which is painting, and I have to finish getting better. It's very important to me."

"Are you sick, Torey?" That idea made sense to him. "Is that why you're leaving? To go to Roma and see the doctors, like I did, and then you'll come back?"

A traitorous tear spilled over the rim of her eye and fell on his sweet face. "Oh, Benedetto, I almost wish it were like that, so easy." She told him simply and briefly about Jon and the accident and the two long years afterward. She deliberately did not talk down to him, using the word *depression* and explaining as fully as she could how many kinds of sickness there were in the world. "Can you understand it a little more now? Why I have to go on and get stronger, better?"

"You won't stay with us because you are afraid, like I am, that we will die or leave you. So, you'll leave us first and escape the hurt it is to love someone." His tone was confident and it staggered her.

"Oh, no," she protested. "I do love you very much. But I have to love myself again, Benedetto. If I am still afraid of losing people, it only shows me I haven't gotten better yet. All through our lives people come and go for lots of different reasons. We can still love them without holding on to them forever."

The boy nodded, unconvinced. His tears had stopped, but he shook all over like a fledgling bird. Torey continued to hold him, rocking him on her lap and kissing the perfect shells of his ears, drawing in the odor of the sea and soap. Andrea came down from the house to find them locked in the embrace and wisely he asked no questions and made no comment at all.

The sea swelled under the boat's blue hull. The three of them, with all the other onlookers, crowded the black, battered rail to watch the Trapanese reenact the timeless catch of the huge tunny schools swimming annually between Africa and Sicily. The carnival air confused Torey; people drank and passed wine about freely, joking carelessly. The wind carried snatches of songs to them and someone on their boat would pick up the melody. All the tourists in town and most of the natives were there, as if it were a circus and not just a catch of fish.

They watched from boats of all sizes from rowboats to yachts, ringing the fleet in a wide semicircle. The fishing smacks were just close enough to allow them to see the individual fishermen clearly but not close enough to impede the fleet's progress. The smacks moved slowly in procession to the point of a watery triangle only they could see. Andrea and Benedetto explained that the nets had been laid down in April, and the pattern, set by tradition, formed a series of narrowing channels and chambers to steer the schools as they passed through Trapani's waters.

"The seventh net out there is called 'the chamber of death,'" announced Benedetto. "All the fish are finally forced into it and that's what we're waiting for now. The *rais,* the head man, will give a signal to the haulers and they'll start to pull it up. More fish than stars in the sky! Tell me when you see the harpooners, Papa. They kill them right away and we have our tuna for the whole year, Torey."

What could she have been thinking of, coming here? Torey shot Andrea a look of sickened bewilderment. Fishing meant a minnow on a hook, a line dangling in the cold waters of Lake Michigan for hours and, just maybe, a small, flopping pan fish to unhook and throw back in. What kind of unfeeling people stood around drinking and singing, enjoying the death of thousands of fish? A sour taste filled her mouth and she was sure she would be physically ill. The press of warm bodies at the rail held her until, in panic, she elbowed her way to the fantail of the boat and sat heavily on a coiled hawser. She trembled and took deep, clean gulps of air.

Andrea's hand pressed suddenly against the back of her head, forcing her to bend her neck. "That's right," he said blandly, "just take in air and the feeling passes quickly. The kill won't start for a few minutes, and you'll feel fine by then."

"Oh, will I?" she hissed through clenched teeth. "Are you insane? What kind of spectacle, Roman circus, is this?" She fought back her nausea and fear with anger. "And to bring a child . . ."

He pulled her to her feet in one motion and said harshly, "What happens here is important and real good, Vittoria! It's been happening every year since men learned to bait a hook and it's part of my world. It's about the real needs of people to work and live and eat, not merely some pretty idea. Sicilians who are hungry don't cry very hard over the gift of food. It's a hell of a lot more sensible to sing and celebrate the death of fish than to sing at the wake of one starved child, don't you think?

"Part of life is death. You and I and Benedetto know it, so why pretend and turn away? Come on back with me and look, really look for once, and think about how beautiful and good the sea is to man when it gives up food for life. If you don't come, you will go on pretending tuna grows in round, neat cans on supermarket shelves. And, perhaps, pretending worse things about life!"

He didn't wait for her answer but took her under one arm and walked her back to the rail, people parting for them and greeting him by name. Andrea thrust her between himself and Benedetto, putting his arm across her back, effectively pinning her there.

"I could close my eyes," she said. But she knew closing her eyes to things was part of the past and didn't help ease the fears. There would be the sounds Benedetto had described and she would know what was happening even in darkness. Most of all, the sense of Andrea's passionate words couldn't be blotted out. He was right; she must not be blinded by fears.

A long, deep sigh drifted to them from the fleet. A tall, dark man who captained the entire flotilla, the *rais,* stood far out on the narrow bowsprit of the lead boat. Lonely, silhouetted against the sky, he raised one arm high over his head in a salute. His single voice sang, a high, piercing wail that carried well over the water and instantly silenced the people around her. No one watching moved, drank or joked now. Only his voice, alone and plaintive, was heard, and the song was haunting and sad in a minor key.

Andrea whispered to her with his mouth pressed gently against her ear, "It's the special song for the tuna, honoring their sacrifice. No one knows where the song comes from or how old it is."

Slowly, one by one, the other fishermen joined the twisting, Arabic melody with a harmony of richness and pain. Men stripped to the waist sang, straining around the capstans, raising the nets with their great weight of fish. Their faces were distorted with the work, but they sang until the song gained strength and echoed all around from water to sky and back again.

The sea boiled and churned with a thick white foam and bright metallic flashes. The tuna came to the surface, fighting and sliding over one another in a frenzied dance. Some would leap high and hang suspended above the net cauldron briefly, then fall back into the trap. As the netting raised and closed, the huge living mass came straight out of the sea like silver flowing in a crucible.

Torey did not pause in her description of the scene to Benedetto when the harpooners moved into position, lining the long rails. She painted the words for the boy's mind as the spearing started, the fish heaved endlessly over shoulders into waiting holds. The foam had been dyed pink and now blood-red with the size of the catch. The dirge faded and disappeared; the only sounds now were the slap of waves on hulls and the wild thrashing of fish and the groans of men pushing themselves to their physical limits.

No one else on the boat spoke, but none objected to Torey's quiet commentary for Benedetto. Andrea's arm had relaxed long minutes before and held her gently around the waist. Her profile was framed by the sky and a lace of mahogany hair. The sea wind had burned her cheeks and brought him the scent of carnations mixed with salt. She was so vulnerable to life, newly discovered, and its emotions. He had to warn himself not to swamp the fragile boat she had launched herself in, trying to control her life again. His sigh, slight but heartfelt, was lost on the wind.

When he thought of her leaving, he felt empathy with the great silver tuna, speared and bleeding. But he wouldn't beg her to stay—he couldn't. There were too many burdens for her if she stayed, and they were his burdens, not hers. No, Torey must go on and do whatever she felt was right without him forcing her into his reality and his world. *I must love her while I can, for as long as I can.*

By late afternoon, the spectators had returned to the quiet harbor. The combination of sea air and the incredible experience of the catch had left them all exhausted. Andrea drove back quickly through town, although Benedetto whined about his hunger, promising the boy a good dinner after a cool bath and a chance to relax.

Torey felt herself strung so tight with tension and so eager to do something to shake off the effects of the strange, raw scenes of the fishing ground that she volunteered to cook. The two males cheered at the offer.

"I didn't think American ladies could cook real food," Benedetto remarked in all innocence.

She tickled him until he begged for mercy and went into the kitchen. Teresa was there, waiting for their return, but she wouldn't answer Torey's friendly greeting.

"I was elected to be chef tonight," Torey said in a final attempt to communicate. "I thought I'd whip up an omelet with whatever you have on hand."

"I am on hand," said Teresa sourly, "and I can

still cook for them. Not so pretty a cook, but I didn't get complaints before now."

"I'm not trying to step on your toes," Torey said briskly, "but I'd like to work in the kitchen, cooking or helping out." She was not in the mood for a Sicilian discussion.

"I don't need your help and neither do they. Signora Gardner, things were fine here until Benedetto came back from school, crying and unhappy. Perhaps you need the signore's help, but I don't think *you* are needed." Teresa hung up her apron and stalked out of the kitchen.

I didn't step on her toes, thought Torey. *I broke her damned leg, by the sound of that remark.* She took out eggs, cheese, herbs and found fresh mushrooms and spinach in the refrigerator. By the time she had grated the cheese and scrambled the eggs, she had pushed Teresa's bitter tone into the back of her mind, but she had not been able to ignore the message. She sliced the mushrooms and washed the spinach, singing her tuneless best. Andrea peeked in, sleek as a seal from his shower, and rummaged through drawers for a corkscrew.

"I sincerely hope, Vittoria, you can cook slightly better than you sing."

She waved the sharpest knife under his nose and reminded him that not all Italians were nightingales, either. "I may not be ready for La Scala, and there were certain fish peddlers in Palermo with a better sense of pitch, but I have spirit."

"Yes," he said, and kissed her firmly on the mouth to end the conversation. He felt the new quality to her kiss immediately. She clung to him tightly and was more eager. Torey's hand touched his face as Benedetto did, memorizing the line of his cheekbone and jaw, chiseled nose, and the sensitive, mobile mouth. Her fingers lingered, warm and scented, on his damp hair and traced the scar on his eyebrow. There wasn't any need for words; he knew why she stored away such touches even as he gathered in the sight and sound of her to remember.

"Vittoria," he whispered in a questioning tone.

The serious mood of the day lifted during the meal. Benedetto awarded her a hug and three kisses for the food, and Andrea proposed a toast "to one American lady who can cook." They both stood and bowed to her, making her laugh at such outrageous flattery. After dinner, Andrea brought a tray with coffee outside and they all sat, their backs to the house's rough wall, to enjoy the heat of the day and watch the sun set.

Benedetto held her hand with a moist, desperate grip. He did not mention their earlier talk on the beach, but when Andrea warned him about bedtime, the boy moved closer to her.

"Perhaps we could go to Erice tomorrow, or the salt marshes and Segesta to see the temple. Maybe Torey will stay here an extra day or two, Papa?"

Her eyes met Andrea's and locked. Hugging the boy, she said, "We have to save some trips for the next time I visit."

While Andrea was putting Benedetto to bed, she stared out into the sea as if the answers were all written there. A moon, round and golden as a wheel of manteca cheese, rolled in and out of dark clouds.

She put Andrea's sweater on and buried her head in the thick, rough wool. The scent of tobacco and aftershave clung to its fibers and surrounded her with his presence. She had come such a long way in a few short weeks, but she saw, in the water's blackness, how far she had to travel to a place and a time that was right, that felt like "home." Teresa had hit a nerve with her blunt words. She wasn't needed here; she was only another stray for Andrea to help. *I have to make the journey all the way back myself, facing everything as it comes. But it is so hard alone.*

The red glow of Andrea's cigar brought her back to reality. She hadn't noticed him come back, but he had seen the pensive expression of her face.

"I'm going in to read awhile, Torey. Will you come in with me, or do you want to sit out a little longer?" He wondered if the day had been too brutal, if he had pressed her too hard to shake off her fears.

Torey didn't want to look at him, fearful she would lose her resolve and throw herself into his strong, safe arms and beg to be held and rocked as she had held his child earlier. *I must be stronger than that,* she decided. "I'll sit and relax awhile here, thanks," she said softly. "I want to think about today." *And tomorrow and the days after that.*

Andrea knew he was not going to sleep; he went through the dark house, looked in at Benedetto, and then walked back to his room to stand at the screens and watch the ocean. He could see her huddled shape in the darkness and wondered if she was asleep. Her quiet disturbed him; it was more resignation than peace. Perhaps at *La Mattanza* he'd finally gone too far. He lit another cigar and paced the bedroom like a trapped animal. When he heard a stifled cry followed by a moan he knew it was her, not Benedetto. His muscles bunched and he started out to be there when her dream ended. Then silence followed and he cursed himself for a fool. He stood there, watching and listening at the door, when she walked down the beach.

She had been dozing, her head thrown awkwardly back. It was not really sleep but flashes of dreams that came and went like the clouds across the moon. Silver fish swam past her and lay bleeding on an expressway thousands of miles away. She saw herself wading in Lake Michigan with a fragile conch shell held to her lips, calling for help. At first she was cold and shivered in the sweater. Then she grew damp and feverish with the visions. Andrea, not Neptune, rose from the lake, naked and tan, and offered her an outstretched hand. He spoke in the dream, but she couldn't hear no matter how she strained. When he turned away, she moved restlessly against the stucco wall, scraping her knuckles and drawing blood. His voice pounded in her head, raised in anger, but she was deaf and frightened. He turned once more and she saw his eyes, wide and cloudy and blind.

Torey's heart pounded madly and she woke as wet as if she had just stepped out of the sea. Her clothes reeked with fear, and she tasted the sweet, coppery taste of blood where she had bitten the inside of her cheek, holding back another scream. No one was on the beach. The moon had paled and moved across the sky. It must be only hours before the dawn and the air was still warm. She got up slowly on unsteady legs and, without a pause, pulled off the damp clothes, letting them drop on the sand. She left on only her silver ring of olive leaves.

Her walk to the water was slow and measured, one foot touching the sand completely, heel to toe, before she lifted the other foot to follow. The wind was from Africa, heavy with its earthy, fertile smell. It caressed her and dried her, whispering in a language she couldn't understand. There was no sudden shock of cold to stop her when she reached the water's edge. The Tyrrhenian welcomed her with a mild touch, rising in soft swells like a warm bath. Torey walked until her feet left the pliant bottom and then she began to swim far out.

It was another world in the sea, in the blackness. A string of tiny, faraway lights bobbed along the sweep of distant harbor, but here it was a complete and perfect darkness where sky and water met in a circle of comfort. She dove down until her lungs burned for air, and then, unsure of direction, she relaxed and rose to the surface slowly. When she threw back her head to clear her vision, an arc of water drops followed the motion, diamonds in the moonlight. The waves hissed as they struck the rocks and flowed back. She felt free, peaceful and loved by the greatest force of all.

He watched the silent, stately walk from the house. Her ivory body seemed remote and beautiful, and she was intent on a deliberate and secret errand. His breath had caught in his throat at the sight. When the waters reached her waist, Andrea had opened the door and stepped out. As the sea encircled her shoulders with dancing lights, he walked quickly down the sloping sands. The thought he had was too terrible to give substance to, so he refused to think anymore. Then he saw her leave the sheltered cove, moving beyond the safety of the beach, and he left his own clothes on the sand and threw himself in after her. He forced himself not to rush his stroke and tire before he could reach her. The distance closed slowly between them and he saw her face, a pale oval, just beyond the inky swells.

Without a sound, she had pushed herself up, and in an arch of white, she dove into the depths. A sheet of fire ran over him and drove him faster, pulling harder and harder until he felt the protest of shoulders, back, legs. The heat of exhausted muscles lit a red blaze in front of his eyes and made his blood sing "faster, faster" to his heart. There was a second of despair and then she surfaced suddenly, only a few feet from him. The water thrown back from her hair fell on him.

Treading the black water and letting his body ease back into a quieter state, Andrea swam next to her. She looked peaceful and composed and very young. Her expression startled him; he knew he had seen that look before, but he could not remember where. He reached for her and she smiled lazily, holding out a moon-pale arm. He wondered if she were completely awake, completely aware it was him. She seemed very distant.

"Let's go back now," he said. When she headed for the beach, he followed closely.

Torey waded out of the sea and stood waiting, unashamed, at the edge, foam licking her feet.

Andrea walked behind her, putting his arms about her and holding her against himself lightly.

"You frightened me very badly just now," he admitted.

"I'm a strong swimmer," she said. "It was wonderful out there being free and new. In a strange way, like being born. . . ." Her voice quivered to a halt when she realized what had frightened him. She turned too quickly, their bodies meeting all along their lengths. "No," she insisted, "I wasn't going to . . . I wouldn't—"

His hand pressed her lips closed and he could not let her finish the sentence. She wanted to tell him about feeling completely alive, but he had stayed the words. The wonder of it was still in her, a languorous good feeling that somehow he must know. She swayed closer, moving gently against him. A shock of heat ran through both their bodies, welding her to him. A groan came from deep inside his chest and she knew he wouldn't leave her tonight. She said his name, leaving him no doubt she knew him and wanted him.

He took his fingers from her mouth and brought his head down to taste the sea on her lips. She was so willing; her tongue lightly moved inside his open, hungry kiss until he drank salt and honey from her kiss thirstily. He wanted to be tender with her, but Torey wound her arms around his neck, whispering his name and feeding a growing urgency to have her.

She was wild and brazen, feeling her body tremble with a need she had never felt so strongly. Whatever she'd known before seemed nothing to the terrible heat that made her cling and move and dig her nails into his shoulders. She knew she was offering herself completely and there was no shame to it, only a delight. When his mouth moved downward, she drew back slightly to allow him more freedom to explore her. When he kissed her breasts gently, she pulled him closer and enjoyed the sound of his ragged breathing. It was the first time she had sensed such a power throbbing deep in her, a power to secretly rule him, even as she became helpless under the whims of his lips and hands.

He knelt before her, a frenzied worshipper, and paid homage to all the hidden, sensitive places of love. She twined one slim hand in his hair and clutched weakly at his massive shoulder for support, sure her bones were no longer solid and trustworthy. Andrea locked his arms around her to keep her from falling on the sand.

"Not here, not this time," he whispered to her. His tongue moved like a hot brand across her stomach. He lifted her up and moved easily toward the house. She found she could not even hold up her head and had to let it rest against the hard planes of his chest. Her hand trailed along the bunched muscles of his arm, enjoying the silken skin that covered such strength.

When she lay in the center of his bed, he looked down at her, a pearl in the darkness. Torey reached out for him, arching her back and moving the delicate ribs into high relief under taut, hot skin. He wanted to content himself and hold his own need in check by looking at her for a while. But she was wiser that night than she had ever been. He could not deny her any pleasure when she called softly to him, saying only his name over and over until he had to take her.

There was a sense of delicious combat to their love tonight. Andrea fought hard to please her before he lost himself, and she struggled harder to conquer him and give him contentment. No one can lose such a war. He let her command him by sighs and gentle movements until her eyes widened, seeing the edge of surrender ahead. Then he fought with a harder, deeper strategy, daring more for more pleasure. He heard her voice dimly through a wild roaring in his head. She whispered yes to him and he lost himself totally in her.

Neither of them spoke afterward, fearful of breaking the spell. They lay together in twisted sheets, touching. He ran his forefinger down her profile and over her throat into the valley between damp breasts and held his hand there until her heart had slowed to a steady, even pace.

"Mia ragazza che risplendi," he whispered softly, thinking she had finally fallen asleep. "My shining girl . . ."

Through her drowsiness she heard him and repeated it to herself. She raised one weighted arm and stroked his face, unable to reply.

"Go to sleep, *bella*," he said, and curled next to her.

She tried to protest. "It's almost light. Benedetto will wake up and . . ."

His kiss silenced her. "I'll worry about him. Sleep here and let me see you in my bed in the morning."

Chapter Eleven

*A*ndrea took his pleasure in watching Torey asleep in his bed. Unfortunately, she opened her eyes to see Teresa out in the hallway, staring at her with a fixed, glittering look. Andrea was nowhere to be seen. Teresa held the clothing, discarded in last night's haste, and just stood there watching with black, eloquent eyes in a white mask.

"Yes?" Torey said, sitting up and drawing the sheet around her. Teresa turned, without answer, into the empty guest room across the hall.

Torey supposed the woman's obvious disapproval was meant to chasten her, but she found she frankly didn't care. She got up quickly, pushing aside the rumpled covers and picking up the pillows strewn on the floor. From the beach, the sounds of laughter and shouts drifted up: Andrea's voice, deep and resonant, followed by Benedetto's higher tenor. She pulled back a corner of the curtain to watch them racing wildly back and forth with a skinny mongrel dog. They were barefoot and wearing jeans, but Benedetto was bundled in a sweater. Nothing seemed different.

She ached pleasantly in the shower. Her breasts were tender as she soaped herself, conjuring up images of the previous night. She had surprised, but not shocked, herself; her lovemaking with Jon had not prepared her for the frenzy she had experienced. The water beat against her, washing away a sense of unreality. Had that wildness, that total surrender, always been hidden deep within her?

Teresa was busy in the kitchen, already preparing lunch. She looked up and gestured at some sliced melon and the coffeepot. It was plain she had made a decision about last night with Sicilian finality. Torey tried to chat casually about *La Mattanza,* asking questions about Gina and Trapani, but every question was answered curtly. Teresa was not going to waste words on such a woman. Increasingly uncomfortable, Torey went out on the beach.

They were still absorbed in their game. Andrea saw her at one point and waved briefly. Childishly, she felt ignored and outside, as if she had already left. She shook herself mentally; no promises or commitments were made on either side last night. Nothing had changed. She, after all, had promised herself not to be derailed from her purpose. Why should it bother her to feel his implacability or Teresa's obvious disapproval of her? Torey called to them.

Benedetto ran over, directed by Andrea and followed closely by the peculiar looking pup. "Do you want to play, too, Torey? Look at this dog! He's really smart, and Papa said if Teresa will feed him while we're gone, I can keep him!"

She knelt down to extend a hand to the brown and white dog. It wagged a furious tail but danced around just outside her reach. "No, Benedetto, thanks. I have to pack this morning for the trip back. He's a nice dog, though, and I'm sure very smart if he picked you. What will you call him?"

Andrea joined them. He reached down and scratched the pup's ears. It rolled over in ecstasy. "Benedetto suggested Neptune, but I argued for Venus. It's more appropriate for a little bitch."

The innocuous remark unaccountably irritated her. Was there always more behind his light tone and dazzling smile than she thought?

Benedetto asked her if she liked the name. Torey replied that if they called the dog Venus, she might well live up to her namesake's reputation and they would have more puppies to contend with before next year.

"The goddess, if I remember my mythology," Torey said, "is apt to bless with fertility as well as love." A wildly disturbing thought crossed her mind as she spoke but she suppressed the notion. "Have you decided when we leave for Palermo, Andrea?"

"I'll have to drive up to Erice this morning," he said. "An old friend of mine lives there and is very ill. I want to visit briefly with him before we leave. Benedetto, don't start to beg! You caught a cold yesterday, I think, and we wouldn't want Uncle

Carlo to catch it. Besides, your ears will ache that high up with a stuffed nose. I'll only stay a half hour with Carlo; he tires very easily now. While I sit with him, Torey, you could look around Erice. . . ."

"Or the temple," Benedetto chimed in. "Then next time can I go and see Carlo?"

"As you like," Andrea replied. "Erice is only a few minutes' drive from here, but you can pack, Torey, if you'd rather wait here."

"When were you planning to leave for Palermo?" repeated Torey, feeling they were talking all around her. "I want to see the Barberas before I go and thank them properly."

"How about this afternoon right after lunch? There's a late plane—about four o'clock. Teresa can warn Peppina to expect us."

"You're taking *her* to meet Don Carlo?" asked Teresa from the kitchen.

Andrea's look silenced the woman immediately. "No," he said, "but only because Carlo is too weak now. Keep an eye on Benedetto while we're gone. I don't want him to go back to school with a fever."

Torey had seen the high promontory of monte Giuliano from the beach but found it hard to believe there was a town perched in such a high and desolate place. Andrea turned the car onto the first of many short, steep grades leading to the mountain's top.

"Who, if I may ask, is Carlo?"

"Carlo Carrara was my classics professor at the university. He's a very distinguished scholar in his field. A year ago, he wrote me from Milan and told me he wanted to move to Erice. He has cancer and not very much time left, so he decided to spend

213

whatever there was left in the place he found most beautiful."

"Is there a hospice there?" she asked quietly.

"No," Andrea said, "no hospice, no hospital. There are only about a thousand people in the whole town. But Carlo said it was sacred ground to him and he wanted it, so I . . . arrangements were made to care for him there. We visit whenever I get back to Trapani and talk about old times."

Torey had caught his slip this time. Andrea had moved his old teacher to Erice. What a complicated man she had met, filled with countless mysteries and secrets. She looked out the window at the sheer drop next to the narrow road and watched a bird flying level with them. The road was still climbing and there were clouds massed below them.

"How high up are we?" she asked. "And why in the world would anyone want to build and live on the top of this rock?"

"It's a very ancient place. For three centuries or more, swarms of people came here to worship at the temple, but now only the hardiest tourists take the cable car and look around. The Phoenicians, Greeks and Romans all used the same temple grounds for their cults of love. I guess whether she was called Astarte, Aphrodite or Venus didn't matter. They came and went, leaving treasures here to pay for her favors or to bribe her. There was a garrison of soldiers on duty here to guard the wealth of the goddess. I imagine that's why they picked such an inaccessible spot."

Torey spotted an eagle gliding effortlessly in the warm updrafts off the cliffs. "She must have been the richest, most powerful lady around, and all that for a promised kiss!"

Andrea laughed. "Well, there were more tangible returns for the gifts. Her servants were temple prostitutes to give the men who worshipped her a taste of physical glory. That's why she was so popular. Does the idea bother you?"

Torey smiled. "Not at all, it's fascinating. I can understand why your friend would be drawn to the place. Is the temple still standing? I thought Benedetto said there was very little left up there."

The road passed through a pine forest, the first Torey had seen anywhere in Italy and particularly striking in nearly treeless Sicily. The fresh scent moved on the breeze, which grew chillier as they drove higher.

"Very little, unfortunately," Andrea explained. "The Normans, who followed the Romans, were a sour, prudish bunch, and they thought the place was an abomination. They destroyed the temple to the ground but kept the place a fortress."

"Some serve love, some serve war," Torey said thoughtfully. "It doesn't surprise me. Sicily seems to have been completely taken over by the Normans' puritanical spirit."

He looked at her quickly and back to the winding road. "Don't believe it! There's a lot of the old goddess left here. That is why Carlo loves Erice so much."

"It seems strange for a dying man to want to be in a place that was devoted to carnality, sexuality." Torey found the scenery beautiful in an alien way. There was a complete silence surrounding them. The birds flew without cries, the wind was still in the pines and the sea lay so far below them there was no sound of waves.

"Venus had many faces and many duties," he said. "Yes, she was love and lust, but nursing mothers came up here to pay tribute to her and old people came to her for comfort. Carlo has a lovely woman born in Erice to care for him, doing her Christian duty and also, unwittingly, serving the goddess. Sicilians say the most beautiful women come from here because they are descendants of the servants of Venus."

"I'm sorry I won't be able to meet Carlo," Torey said. "This sounds fantastic and wonderful, if a little spooky. I don't think I'd like to live in a place full of so many phantoms, happy or not."

The town square was so steeply sloped that Torey imagined the people would slide down its clean, cobbled surface in a high wind. There were few townsfolk on the streets, no barking dogs and no lines with fresh wash hanging from the gray medieval walls. The houses were set back from the streets with tiny enclosed courtyards filled with sunshine and flowers. It was a postcard place; the cleanest place she had seen in Italy and also, curiously, the most lifeless. The silence was overpowering. Erice made Trapani seem like a bustling metropolis.

Andrea parked at a stone house near the far end of the tiny town and gestured at the building. "Carlo lives here, overlooking the old temple site near that headland cliff. From his bed, he can see the field where the temple once stood. I wish you could meet him, but it embarrasses him to receive visitos now."

"It's okay," Torey assured him. "I'll find the place myself, and you come find me after your visit. Are there any markers to look for?"

"There's an old caretaker, but he won't be of much help. Look around for some large flat stones that were the floors. There's nothing else really to go by."

Caretaker? Torey wondered if the caretaker was a ghost when she saw the field completely overgrown with summer grasses, wildflowers and a profusion of wild rose bushes, thick and squat, with masses of small pink flowers and a heavy, cloying fragrance. The sharp thorns caught on her skirt, slowing her progress through the weeds. Insects buzzed, but there were no birdsongs from the trees. The place was lovely, drenched in bright sunshine, but it too had the feeling of an alien plain about it. She told herself she had listened to Andrea's history too carefully.

An old man was tending some spindly tomato plants down the short slope to her right. He was bent into a fishhook by arthritis, and she saw his spotted, gnarled hands like wooden roots move with infinite patience among the leaves. He saluted her approach by tipping a straw hat.

"My plants are flowering, signorina, but they set no fruit yet," he said without a preamble of greeting, as if they were old friends.

"They should do very well here, though," Torey answered, trying to file away his face for a drawing later. "May I just walk through the field for a while?"

He waved her on, busy again with his plants. "It's good to visit her."

A broken tooth of stone protruded from a stand of waist-high grass. She waded through and saw the entire sweep of Sicily's west coast and even a purple smudge that might have been Africa. Trapani was clear down to the tiny red-tiled roofs. She had the sense of seeing the ancient world at her feet, the view the goddess had had long ago.

This place was not neglected, she realized in sudden insight. No one would profane the spot by cutting down the earth's tributes to her, whether they were flowers or grasses. Whatever the season brought, it was left as a token for the goddess. Torey's foot touched a smooth spot and she knelt down, pushing aside the weeds. A gray slab, warm as a beating heart, lay under her fingers. Hidden and wind-worn to a glassy finish, the rock was part of the temple's floor.

She found she had tears in her eyes. The field was only a mountain pasture, the flowers perfectly ordinary and the stones only flat, eroding slabs. She had seen so many impressive ruins, it was peculiar that this nothing of a temple in the middle of nowhere should have any effect at all. But Torey wanted to stay and hold her fingers on the stone, feeling in it a timeless peace and goodness. The funny little roses were everywhere, creeping long runners and climbing around stone fragments of walls. A bed of roses, she thought. She broke off a spray and held it tentatively in her hand, enchanted by the delicacy but wary of the red thorns.

She settled herself on the ground, letting her hand keep contact with the floor stone, and rested against a boulder. A sense, an intuition filled her and she knew what she must do, but it seemed crazy! She waited, concentrating on the hum of cicadas and the flight of swifts overhead. She should not have taken the roses; it was like chipping off pieces of the Coliseum for a souvenir. She put the flowers into her skirt pocket apologetically. Crazy or not, Torey dug out a small hole next to the stone, scratching with her fingernails, took off her silver ring and put it firmly down into the rich, dark earth. Then she carefully replaced the dirt and patted it down firmly. Unsure whether she was happy or sad, she cried for a few minutes, feeling a blend of emotions without words to explain it.

Andrea called her name, looking for her. He found her quickly although she hadn't bothered to answer. His eyes looked a deeper blue, a sadness there at seeing his old friend, and the corners of his mouth were set and tight, tired with talking trivialities in the face of Carlo's death. Torey tipped her head to one side slightly and looked up at him with mild, almost mocking eyes. Her mouth was sweet but unsmiling.

"I want you, Andrea," she said, surprising herself. "I want you now."

If he had said "Not here," she would have been relieved. If he had said "You must be crazy," she would have agreed and left. If he had said anything at all, she knew she would not have had the courage to love him once more before she left. But he went to her, kneeling down and drawing her to himself without a word, as if it was the most natural and reasonable thing in the world.

There was no haste or sense of desperation. They

touched and kissed and held each other in slow, devoted ways. Andrea paid her beauty gentle tribute, lingering over her mouth and throat, the curve of her shoulder and breast. She whispered to him, unashamed to tell him what she wanted. He offered her one gift after another until she demanded his hard, lean body. Then, she felt that only the unyielding stone under her kept her from dissolving and melting into the earth. Nothing existed but the warmth of his body on hers, the strength of his arms and legs, and an endless motion carrying her higher than the top of a lonely mountain.

He was dizzy with the scent of the roses clinging to their bodies and called her name over and over with words muffled by her hair and flesh. They were welded, bone on bone, skin to skin, and made a single, final sacrifice to love together.

She felt clumsy, even awkward afterward. It would have been heavenly to stay there and sleep a while, wrapped in his arms. She forced buttons through buttonholes, angry at her slow fingers, frightened at her unpredictable moods. Andrea helped her to her feet, brushing long strands of grass from her hair, and they walked slowly back through the field. The old man was still there, watering his seedlings, and as they passed he smiled warmly and nodded.

Andrea drove through the town and onto the mountain road before he spoke. His voice was husky and low. "You know, Vittoria, you don't have to go," he said slowly.

She thought about it for a few minutes. He hadn't said, "I don't want you to go," or more precisely,

"Stay!" He was, as ever, honest. She knew she didn't have to go. She could stay and he would be there. But it was not what she should do, what she must do.

"No, I can't stay any longer. You and I talked this out in Palermo," Torey said finally. "I can always come back, I suppose."

"Any time," he said in a strong, almost stern tone. "I want you to promise me you will call or write me if there is anything—"

"You've done everything," Torey interrupted, "and more than anyone else could have. How could I possibly ask you for more?"

He stopped the car promptly in the middle of a switchback and turned to her. His face was smooth Greek sculpture, but the scar on his eyebrow flushed with an inner struggle. "I'm not leaving here until I have your promise you will ask for my help, only mine, if you need it." His eyes were blue ice, cold and unyielding.

"You're frightening me," Torey said. "Yes, I promise. Please, Andrea, let's go."

On the drive back to Trapani he told her a little about his visit with Carlo. His friend was, indeed, much worse, and it was understood there weren't many visits left. Torey wondered if he was feeling guilty, making love after such a painful visit, but she wouldn't ask him. There seemed to be an unspoken agreement between them not to discuss what had happened.

Benedetto was waiting, impatient to see them. He sniffled and jabbered about the marvels of the puppy while Teresa brought in lunch, a scowl cutting trenches in her stoic face. Except for the boy, who seemed marvelously unaware of everything but his new pet, the others had to try and ignore a cloud of tension and stress that surrounded the meal.

"We'd better leave right after this," said Andrea. "Benedetto should get back before Sister Veronica writes him off as a truant. You can see Peppina and make the plane, Torey, if we hurry." He looked at her for signs that she might relent, but her jaw was firmly set and her eyes were green marble.

"I'll be ready in ten minutes. Jon always said my one virtue was punctuality. That was only because my father had the nasty habit of leaving us kids wherever we were if we weren't ready to go when he was. I missed my high school graduation because I was upstairs agonizing over my hair." She laughed and realized it hadn't hurt at all. She had mentioned Jon as casually and naturally as she would have spoken of Peppina or Paola. It hadn't choked her into silence.

Teresa set down a plate of hot rolls with a thump and said piously, "In Sicily, a woman's only virtue is modesty." The cruel remark hung in the air between them with the steam from the plate.

Torey snapped, "How very dull for you women. If you have no other virtues, though, I suppose you might as well be modest!"

Andrea warned Teresa, "She's a sharp-tongued one, too. Tread carefully or be prepared for a fight."

Teresa contented herself with shooting another angry look that Torey thought of privately as the "Sicilian dagger" and went back to work.

The good-byes were slightly protracted because Benedetto had to give Teresa very detailed instructions on the care and feeding of Venus. He was eager to find a book in Braille on training dogs before his yearly vacation. He hugged the dog until it squealed before getting reluctantly into the car. Andrea formally shook hands with Teresa and then playfully pinched her cheek, reminding her to call him with any problems.

Torey stepped forward and would have offered the woman her hand but she was met with a curt nod. Teresa hurried back into the house before anything further could be said. Driving away, Torey finally expressed her surprise at Teresa's open hostility and cool attitude. She asked Andrea how she had offended the woman so deeply.

"You have to forgive a lot in her, Torey, as we do," he said. "Her husband was lost last year in a storm and it soured her badly. Staying here in Trapani is not good for her or for Gina, but she's too stubborn to leave and I won't dismiss her, no matter how difficult she is."

"This is a nation of widows, isn't it?" Torey commented as Trapani disappeared behind them.

Words formed but Andrea choked them back. Benedetto sitting between them was the best censor in the world. *Widow* meant empty and defeated; she was his shining girl, full of warmth and light.

The traffic became impossible as they approached the sprawl of Palermo. Benedetto grew quieter and pensive as they neared the school. Noticing his unhappiness, Torey fumbled in her bag and brought out the small white box she had wrapped for him. She pressed it into his hand without explanation.

He opened it slowly, feeling through the cotton carefully, and brought out the red coral horn she had bought such a short time ago. He touched it, judging the material and shape, and smiled up at her. "To ward off the evil eye? Is it white or red coral, Torey?"

"Red," she said. "Red as your runny nose, as the sun setting over Trapani, and as red as my face got when I tried to speak Sicilian."——

"It's good luck for me. I'll always wear it and nothing bad can happen. Thank you, Torey," he whispered, slipping it inside his white school shirt. "I won't let the sisters see it. They don't like pagans."

Torey tickled him. "And don't tell them about our conch shell, either. I'll never blow it when mother superior is around."

"What's all this nonsense?" asked Andrea.

"Secrets, Papa, between Torey and me."

"Well," sighed Andrea with a long look at her over the boy's head, "she can trust secrets to a Sicilian. We're the most secretive, silent people on earth."

"Honorable about secrets, *si*, but silent? Never!" Torey laughed with a full heart.

Benedetto insisted Torey come into school to say good-bye. She was not sure her control would hold if he cried or begged her not to go. But he was relaxed, angelic and seemed very happy, kissing her hand and giving her one last hug. He touched the charm under his shirt and nudged her in conspiracy. She promised him solemnly that if she could come back soon, she would, and she knew he believed her. More than those few words she could not promise.

Andrea had seemingly read her inner turmoil. On the way to via Emma, he said, "Benedetto trusts you, Vittoria. I hope you were not trying just to be kind by promising a visit and then being cruel when you can't fulfill the promise."

"I didn't lie to him," she said. "I'll be back to Palermo again, I'm sure."

"Don't let your Roman friends think you yearn for us," he said sarcastically. "They will think you have been bewitched if you say anything good of poor, barbaric Sicily."

"I don't have anything but good to say," Torey replied softly. "Now I can go on, I can paint again, laugh and be happy. A lot of those things came about because of you and Benedetto and you know it. I only wish I had a gift for you to express my gratitude."

Then give me yourself forever, he almost said impulsively. *Stay!* But he didn't. He had made his choices long ago, and now he was bound to see them through, no matter the cost. Torey would not be happy here, locked into his choices and forever wondering what lay beyond Sicily for her. The feelings she had for him would turn to resentment, perhaps to hatred, and he could not survive that. No, it was better not to ask and still have the dream.

"We both had treasures enough from you, Vittoria," he said, slightly hoarse. "What of the future, *cara?*"

She wished she could read his mind, fathom the subtle, shifting moods of this man. Did he feel an obligation to help her because of what had been between them briefly, because of his child's feelings for her? She wasn't going to be another of his many personal obligations, his problem children.

"A very wise Sicilian told me to accept what was, what is and what will be. It seems like the best advice right now." She wondered how long it would be before he had another lost or troubled person to help. He'd be keeping his old promises to Scarpi over and over in his own extraordinary way. She was only too aware of how soon she'd be out of his life.

Peppina's farewell was emotional and weepy. Betta snorted constantly and begged to go to the airport to make a scene at the departure gate. Andrea threatened her with a beating if she didn't stop sniveling, so she retreated to the corner, moping. Peppina alternated between clutching Torey to her birdlike ribs and scolding her for leaving too soon.

"I'm going to Rome myself when Paola's baby is due, and then I'll take care of you, too. Who will see that you eat right? Torey, stay until Christmas when I go. Andrea, I appeal to you to make the woman see some sense! Has she painted the last stick or stone of interest in Palermo?" Peppina pointed at him as final judge.

Andrea stood at the mantel, looking at the sketches of Betta. "Vittoria does what she thinks is best, not what you think. That's best!"

Peppina shook her fist at him. "You idiot." She sneered. "I should have known better. Much you know about anything! I know what I know. You are a pair of donkeys fit for one cart or . . ."

At that quip, Andrea made a quick expressive gesture to her that Torey did not see. It said more than volumes of writing and Peppina shut up, aware she was on very treacherous ground.

After more bone-snapping hugs and tearful promises that Betta would write letters for all of them, Torey pulled herself away. Gian-Carlo and Beppo suffered a few kisses and ran after the car, waving wildly.

"I hate airports," Torey shouted over the noise of the milling travelers, "and bus stations always make me cry."

They waited until the plane was boarding the last stragglers. Torey juggled her purse and a paper bag of fruit Peppina had insisted she take.

"I must go now, Andrea," she said, taking her hand from his grip. "The plane will leave any minute."

"Do you know Latin?" he asked her suddenly.

She laughed at the odd question. "High school variety only." *Amo, amas, amat . . . I love, you love . . .*

"When Carlo and I were talking, he reminded me of a quotation. *Vincit qui se vincit.*"

"He conquers who conquers himself," she translated without difficulty. "Is that the thought I should leave on?"

"Yes," he said with a finality in his voice. His eyes were the color of the Tyrrhenian in sunlight. "Good-bye, Vittoria, and be happy, my shining girl." He put a light kiss in the palm of her hand and closed her fingers over it tightly.

The plane taxied out while he stood and watched. He went through the mobbed terminal quickly and realized he didn't mind going back to Peppina's. Her torrents of accusations and heaps of abuse were preferable to being alone with himself tonight.

Chapter Twelve

Torey had stopped at Paola's for her mail. It still came to the Vizzinis' apartment for the sake of convenience. When she had tried to have it forwarded to her tiny new studio, the postal clerk had told her it would be six months to a year before the change would be effected. He was not in the least apologetic; after all, she spoke Italian, wore Roman fashions and looked at home here. Surely she knew the problems of the Italian mails. Every few days, Torey ran over to Paola's to pick up her mail.

She had been more than just busy in the last two weeks. The small studio was not far from the Termini station, and after one look, she had rented it, ignoring the loudest and best objections from Paola and Roberto. Torey loved the busy working-class neighborhood filled with foreign laborers and crowded shops, and she had failed to make them understand why she could not paint as happily in the Vizzini chrome-and-glass studio. It reminded her of a hospital operating room, she said, and her tarps looked out of place over the parquet floors.

Three days after renting it, Torey moved in a cot and hot plate and Paola had thrown up her hands in disgust. It no longer made sense to live in the huge apartment with them and trek daily to the studio and, more frequently, to the gallery. There seemed to be endless details to work out with Viviano before the showing. Now she worked eight to ten hours a day and longer, if she wanted. To placate Paola, she visited every weekend. To satisfy Viviano, she was turning out more material for the show. To keep Roberto happy, she was charming to his law partners at the dinner parties. To stay sane, she allowed herself to think about Andrea only once or twice a day.

"Tell me," said Paola with artificial brightness, "have you heard from anyone lately?"

Torey wasn't fooled; she had learned her lessons in Palermo. "Yes, in fact, I have. My father sent me a letter of credit from the insurance settlement. I'm paying for Betta's sewing machine and it will be delivered to via Emma this week. My secret admirer, Gaspare Viviano, sent me another mash note proclaiming his undying affection and total faith in my talent, and he hinted at dark designs on my body. Benedetto dictated a letter to Sister Angela in English about animal training for Venus and complaining about Francesca. He pursued her so long, and now he's discovered she doesn't like detective stories."

"No one else?"

"Betta wrote for Peppina. They are all sure I've faded into a wraith without their cooking. Betta saw Robert Redford in a movie and wants to know how she can meet him."

Paola was infuriated by this point. She screamed, "Don't be deliberately thick, Victoria. I meant Scarpi and you know it! Has the friendly philosopher written to you yet?" She had given up smoking for the baby, but Torey made her nervous. She hunted through the table drawers for the cigarettes she had made Roberto throw away.

"I haven't heard a thing," said Torey. "I'm sure he's much too busy to write. Besides, what would he say? 'It was lovely arguing with you, having you make my child a little nuts, listening to all your problems?'" He was in Taormina this week, London next week. By the time the show closed, he'd be in Trapani with Benedetto, throwing sticks for Venus.

"Don't be this way," said Paola, slamming the drawer shut. "I hate when you try to be brittle and gay because you are so bad at it."

Torey shrugged her shoulders and stuffed the letters in her purse. "I'm on my way to via del Barbuino to see what Viviano wants to do about hanging the paintings. I'm not going to squabble with you and then go and fight with him. Do you need anything from the piazza del Spagna?"

"You're a treasure, Torey! I have a tiny list of things for the dinner tomorrow, and really, I'm dead tired all the time. I don't have the energy to get half these things done. Fabrizio is coming, by the way, so don't you pretend to forget and make me send Roberto to get you."

Torey groaned, "Oh, no, not him. If he bursts into *Pagliacci* over dessert, I'll strangle him."

"He likes you," insisted Paola hopefully, "and he has a nice voice, don't you think?"

What Torey thought she did not say. It was more difficult to hold her temper, not easier, since the trip. She was charged with frantic energy, always on the go, while Paola had sunk into a blissful lethargy, designing at the office for two hours in the morning and then enjoying the rest of the day. It was uncanny, as if they had exchanged habits. Paola cried at the slightest provocation while Torey had a very casual attitude toward everything but her work and Fabrizio's impromptu opera concerts.

Gaspare Viviano was worried, however. He had made a life's work of anxiety and he was not about to relax now. He dragged Torey into the gallery's storage area and pressed his cheeks in typical anguish. She knew the gesture and waited for the heart-rending speech which had to follow. It only meant Viviano wanted some important concession from the artist.

He was an old tyrant, a bald-faced and charming liar and scrupulously honest about his commissions. Torey frankly adored him and would have taken his florid love notes more seriously if he were not seventy-three, four times a grandfather and madly in love with his wife, Amelia, who bullied him unmercifully. Today she thought he was in particularly good form, playing out his scene perfectly. He squeezed out a few real tears so that, in the end, she promised him six more paintings and his exclusive handling of another show in a year.

"I will have you dragged through the streets, beautiful child," he said, gleefully wiping his eyes, "right into court if you let another person sell so much as your shopping lists. Also, I think five percent more in commission on the next show would be about right." He folded his hands across his ulcer and smiled wolfishly at her, sure of himself.

"Then you'll get nothing, you miserable old fraud," said Torey with a smile of her own. "I promised you paintings, the next show and nothing else. Nothing! You and I both know you are going to serve cheap champagne next month, encourage Paola and Roberto's friends to hail you as the discoverer of fresh talents, and you will sell my work at our old, agreed upon, commission."

The old man looked mortally wounded. He was, in fact, thinking about his lunch and deciding tortellini with cheese really would sit better on his stomach. When the pose got no response from her, he pulled out all the stops.

"I meant to tell you right after you got back from Palermo how divine you look, but money worries have pressed me so. Now, you are always lovely to me, you know, but lately you are transfigured! I saw the beauty in you and in the paintings as two aspects of one experience, let me tell you. I even bought you a very small, insignificant gift at Fratelli Biondi to let you know I appreciate your secret."

Viviano rummaged through his tangle of cabinets

and pressed a large, flat envelope into her hands. He beamed, confident he was on the trail of a full five percent more without compromise. Torey opened it and found an expensive, excellent reproduction of Botticelli's famous *Birth of Venus*. The gift impressed her but she confessed she didn't have a clue as to what he meant.

"You were there and you saw her," he said slyly. "Paola was in right after you returned and told me herself. Torey, she said, has been to Trapani. I looked at all the paintings again and of course"—he tapped the side of his nose—"I knew what that meant."

Torey scrutinized the elegant picture for clues. Venus stood gracefully on her gold-rimmed shell above the turbulent waters, her long unbound hair blowing with wind. Spirits hovered about her and small pink roses floated through the air. No help there.

"All right," said Torey, bowing to his sneaky genius. "I'm intrigued and still ignorant. What does this all mean?"

"It's a compliment," hissed Viviano. He was incensed she hadn't capitulated immediately. What was a few thousand lire between friends? "You saw her and she gave you the touch of greatness, no? Her love pours like the sea from your new work. Amelia and I have been there and waded in the sea, looking up to her home on monte Giuliano. You swam to her rock where she was born." He tapped the reproduction for emphasis. "And as one great beauty to another, the deal was made." He brushed his hands together wildly, indicating the conclusion of a successful business deal.

Torey was bewildered and repeated dully, "I went to Trapani to meet Venus and bargain with her?"

"Oh, Torey, don't tease an old man," he moaned. "I'm not a pagan to believe that old load of rubbish; but I know the legends, and the work speaks for itself. It could almost have been true, my dear, when I saw these." He swept his hand around the room, where everything she'd done was propped, framed, ready to be hung.

Small pieces of a puzzle formed slowly in her mind but she couldn't tell what they meant. "You said 'a touch of greatness,' and I heard that before. In Sicily, as a matter of fact."

Viviano gave up in disgust. He had tried to bribe her, paying her an ultimate compliment, and she still had not begged him to take more money.

"Venus was born in the sea below the rock we call monte Giuliano. You can't have missed it!" He said each word slowly, enunciating as if she were a rather dull child. "There is even an old temple there at Erice. Now, the crazy people who inhabit that island think she can still gift them with love and beauty. Lots of equally crazy—a thousand pardons—artists and musicians go there so she can touch them with her power. That's it, the whole pretty story.

"Except that three or three and a half years ago, a pretty American student at the Academy painted me a pretty landscape now and then. One day this summer, Paola Vizzini comes in, wild-eyed, with a handful of pastels and sketches. I looked at them and

I loved them. Who wouldn't? They were alive, fresh and new. She told me, in perfect seriousness, Vittoria Gardner did them, and everyone says *I* lie! I couldn't believe it, not from the little girl who made such neat and delicate landscapes."

Torey felt frozen to the floor. Hearing the story made the gallery's familiar interior fade away. She saw a woman swimming naked in the warm Tyrrhenian sea on a very black night. She glanced down to the Botticelli and then to Viviano mopping his hands off on his handkerchief.

"Forgive me," concluded Viviano, "but I thought it was only a fluke. You hadn't worked in so long I imagined you were only trying out something new. I didn't suppose it would last, but then the paintings arrived and each one was better than the last. I shouldn't be saying this before we sign a contract, but perhaps I've gone totally mad, as well. *Children of Sicily, Peppina Laughing,* all the ones of La Mattanza . . . They are superb!"

She saw only herself on a beach, damp hair in long strands on her shoulders and back. Andrea's forearms, bunched with muscle, tried to hold her upright, and she recalled the open, raw hunger for him that had seemed so right, so alien, all at once. Torey turned to walk out holding Viviano's gift.

"Victoria? The new contract?"

"Three percent more and no further discussion," she said. "Six paintings by the end of next month, if possible. Please order some decent wine, Gaspare, for once in your long life. And my thanks for the gift. Let it be our little secret."

She could not remember how she got to her

studio. She found herself there studying the Botticelli propped against a wall. Torey looked at Venus with a sense of awe and wonder, although she had seen the painting many times before. It had never been more than a lovely work blending classicism and paganism until now.

She looked at it as a clue in the treasure hunt she had started here in Rome and leading to a goddess's birthplace. The long search for herself was somehow tied to this masterpiece, and it was a comic stroke to have Viviano, that crafty businessman, hand it to her.

Venus looked back at her, tipping her head slightly. The other figures stared at the goddess, but Venus looked straight ahead with mild, mocking eyes. Her sweet mouth was at the edge of a smile because she knew a secret. *I'm sitting here,* Torey thought with disgust, *puzzling over a painting as if it were a road map to happiness. This is strange, bordering on crazy, and not a direction I want to go in. Hello, Venus, for a short time I think I was you.* She promptly faced the reproduction to the wall, refusing to look at it anymore.

She decided to try to finish six paintings in four weeks. Torey had never worked under such pressure before. It meant painting directly on the canvas without bothering to sketch. The paintings grew in big, flat areas of color, like giant posters, and then she went back, detailing and refining each one. The new colors she used were bright and violent on the palette—reds, violets, greens and yellows vibrating before her eyes—but once on the canvas, they looked right and controlled. The size of the paintings had grown too, as if she needed more space to contain these bigger ideas.

She painted Benedetto's face against the roughness of black rock, one hand offering the viewer the very same conch shell she had set on her work table. She painted an old man watering his tomatoes who she had only seen twice. She painted a portrait of Andrea as she remembered him at Trapani. It had the look of elusive peace she hadn't forgotten. It did not flatter him, and he would like that, she knew.

There were moments when her hand trembled over the handsome, angular planes of his face, and Torey knew it was not merely fatigue. It was too hard to match his skin tone to a memory and to avoid the other thoughts that rushed in. She turned away from his painted eyes, knowing how the real eyes looked at her.

She began one with no particular plan. A pale figure took shape and became a slender woman walking across a brown beach. The woman carried a large sheaf of golden wheat, and behind her, stretching into the distance, there were single stalks planted in one straight row just beyond the force of the waves. The painting became her Venus.

When the studio had become a jumble of completed and half-finished pictures, Paola dropped by. Torey realized with a start she had been working day and night for nearly two weeks. Evidently, Paola had realized it, too; she was not her usual agreeable self.

"I'm coming to check up on you every day," she announced. "Frankly, I thought you had fallen off a ladder and were lying here with a broken neck.

Twice, not once, Viviano bearded me in my own apartment, wanting to know why you haven't answered his notes, why you don't have a telephone, and if you ran away. Something *is* wrong, isn't it? What aren't you telling me?"

"I'm not telling you anything because"—Torey put down her brush—"you have talked without stop for ten minutes. I am sorry I missed your dinner, but I won't be there tonight either. There's a week, Paola, to the show, and I don't have time to be pleasant and social. Frankly, I feel so nasty and antisocial I wouldn't want anyone to see me."

"Well, you look fine, although I don't see how. I'm determined to change your mind about Capri, however. If I tell Roberto it's settled tonight, he'll make all the arrangements for you—tickets, schedule, all the details he thrives on. It would be a marvelous place for you to rest completely after this."

Torey wavered. "Yes . . . Paola, wait! Maybe I should go, but don't ask me for an answer now. Do me one favor more and keep Viviano amused until next Wednesday night. You can come over if you have to and make sure I haven't hung myself in the rafters, but really, no parties with sincere, panting lawyers and no fights with Gaspare."

Paola giggled like a little girl. "They mean well, *cara,* and everyone is being driven mad by your air of mystery."

"It's boredom and sheer exhaustion," Torey said. "In six more days, no matter what, I'll quit. You and I can go shopping, I'll have my hair done, I'll drink gallons of Viviano's champagne and be witty and pleasant to everyone. Then I'll think of hibernating for a while."

Paola was convinced that Torey had never looked so well since her return; she glowed with some inner light, regardless of how tired she was. She looked as young and bright as she had years before, her face thin but without the pinch of sadness. There was nothing substantial for Paola to go on; Torey had been deliberately vague in discussing what had happened in Trapani. What had been unsaid was more significant than what she had said, and Paola could read signs as well as an old hunting guide. When Torey concentrated her energies, worked possessed with purpose and began avoiding the weekends with them, Paola insisted to Roberto that Torey was in love. "I know that look" was her final summation.

He had told his wife, in his best courtroom manner, not to interfere and arrange matters, no matter how strong Paola's suspicions were. He talked about circumstantial evidence, saying, "It's *her* life, Paoletta, and she has grabbed it back with both hands. If you poke around it with those long fingers, you'll make a mess. Let her be!"

Paola strolled over to the unfinished portrait of Scarpi and ran her long fingers over the nailheads on the side. She caught an inquiring look from Torey.

"I called Peppina last night," said Paola, "and asked her to send Betta on ahead this September. We'll let her have your old room and I can use her in the studio immediately. There's no reason she should wait until Peppina and the boys come after the baby. Betta understands she's going to do the simplest, lowest work for a start, but it could go somewhere." She tried to think of a way to get Torey to *talk* about this man, not paint him.

Torey resumed painting, growing a little resentful of the time Paola was taking up. Her slim reserve of patience was dwindling rapidly. "That's nice. I wonder who will manage the building when Peppina leaves. Andrea relied on her so heavily to keep things running smoothly. I can imagine he wasn't too pleased with this idea of their moving."

"What a simpleton you can be, Torey! As I understand it, Scarpi urged them to accept our offer. He's offered to send the boys to a good school here in Rome; it seems he wanted to all along, but Peppina had fought him. The older son is doing well, she told me."

"Aldo is in Agrigento," said Torey, and gave up any hope of painting. She sat on the edge of the cot with Paola, who promptly stretched out for a rest. Torey picked up the tiny conch and turned it over and over in her hand.

Paola suggested Torey was homesick and might fly home to Chicago. Her comment was met with an eerie silence. Torey seemed oblivious to her, to the sounds of the children playing shrilly in the street below, to everything but the shell she held. It convinced Paola, circumstantial or not, that Torey Gardner was holding back a secret, and she was just as sure she could help.

Finally and quietly, Paola said, "I'm not leaving here until I know what's bothering you and what you are not telling me. Would you tell me, Torey, if you are pregnant?"

The smile Paola got in answer was sad and bleak. "No," Torey said, "I'm not pregnant." The moment she had known, surely and without question, that she would not have Andrea's child had crushed a wordless, formless hope for her. Venus doesn't give all her gifts so easily.

"But I love him," she admitted with wise, resigned eyes. "You seemed to know it before I did."

When had she known it? She realized the pace she was setting for herself was a killing one, meant to block out thoughts of him. Except for the brief moments between wakefulness and sleep, Torey had not allowed herself to think about Andrea Scarpi. But she followed a tall, dark man near the Spanish Steps one day because his thick black hair had curled a certain way over his collar. She had cried at the cleaners when a few dried brown roses had slipped out of her skirt pocket.

It was a tremendous relief to tell Paola. The gaps in her story explained themselves and those things which were too private to be spoken of to anyone didn't stop Paola from understanding that something beautiful, almost mystic, had happened in Trapani.

Paola asked, "And so? What do you do next?"

Torey smiled. "That, of course, is the only question left. I don't know because I haven't allowed myself time to think about the problem, let alone a solution. Maybe there isn't one."

"Roberto swears the only solution to love is marriage, which he claims can cure the worst case." Paola laughed. "Except naturally, in his own case. He tells me he is the happiest man in the world."

"Andrea doesn't have marriage in mind. He has

enough problems without taking on another, permanent obligation."

"You're impossible," snapped Paola. "You are not a problem to anyone but yourself, never have been. And this man should have made you see that!"

"Oh, I think he did," exclaimed Torey, "but you missed the point! He helps people in a compulsive way. He felt sorry for me, I'm sure. Why should I let myself think there was more to it than that?" Torey paced around the studio, agitated by the pain these thoughts produced.

Paola pointed to the Botticelli hidden against the wall. "That's why and you know it. A man doesn't love a woman out of a sense of pity, Torey. You went there sad, inert, almost useless as a woman and an artist; you met this man, and you're more now than you ever dreamed possible. I know who's blind, and it's not Benedetto. I can't speak for Scarpi, but if you feel this way about him, you should find a way to tell him. You're not a Sicilian, bound up by pride and tradition. You're a woman with love at stake."

"I can picture him at Cefalu," Torey said, "shaking me up so badly or being cool and distant, and it makes me cringe inside. Facing him and telling him how I feel might be terrible, as bad as losing Jon." She turned her head away from Paola's sympathetic look. "Because he's alive, and if he won't have me, I'll have to go on knowing that."

Torey gave in to the feeling and let herself enjoy the relief of tears. They were not angry or bitter tears, but they still burned on her cheeks and made her throat ache.

Paola held her tightly and mopped her face as in

practice for her own child. "Come on, you think only about the show now and its success. Let your divine friend Venus do her work. You'll know what to do when this nonsense is over."

The gallery on the via del Barbuino was tightly jammed with lookers, browsers, buyers and friends. Viviano felt dapper in his best blue suit, cut for a much younger man, and spent a good deal of the evening admiring his reflection in the glassed sketches. Seven pictures sold in two hours and he gloated, thinking of how many more would be gone before the wine ran out. He offered up a short, silent prayer of gratitude that Amelia was home with migraine, that he would soon have a new gilt-edged sign out front and, finally, that his artist was not a doddering wreck like himself and would produce many more shows like this one. He adjusted the knot in his silk tie, using a pastel of an aggressive Palermo postcard vendor for a mirror.

"My girl." He caught at Victoria's arm and pulled her to his side. "Don't avoid me on our night of nights! Over there are some important people I promised to introduce you to. They want to talk about buying *Children of Sicily* for a sum so vast"—and his arms described wild circles to encompass all the money in the world—"and a future commission for a new hospital. . . ."

Torey bent down to his papery cheek, sweet with lavender, and kissed him lightly. "I'll talk about the commission, yes. The painting, you already know, is not for sale; I'm giving it away soon. Now, go sell all the rest and take Amelia away for a nice holiday with my love for you both. Not that painting, though. Where is Paola? I've been looking for her for the last hour."

"She is huddled in my office—my *private* office— on my telephone. That woman talks more than my beloved wife, and tonight of all nights, when she should be sharing the triumph with us!"

All artists were a mystery, Viviano thought as Torey pushed her way through the crowd. He had been in the business of dealing with them for thirty-seven years and had yet to find one he understood. Torey was better than most and far better than he dared hope for. He ran his gaze over the walls with the rich tapestry of color. Her paintings glowed like Byzantine jewels, alive with feeling. He had been frightened the last few weeks when he thought she was verging on a breakdown again, but tonight everything seemed good, even the things he couldn't understand. Had she said she was giving away a painting?

Torey drank one glass of wine after another, thirsty with tension and the heat of the narrow room. Her thirst for praise was sated and there were too many people, too much hugging and kissing, too much talking to critic and buyer. The Frascati wine was smoother and cooler than the usual sour champagne. She solemnly promised herself she would never work this way again; tonight she was sure the paintings would never stop, the ideas would not dry up. There would never be the need to drive herself so hard. If she could ever find Paola, she would tell her what she had decided to do.

"You are radiant, happy and a little drunk, I

think," said Roberto, slipping his arm around her waist.

"Guilty on all counts, counselor, but can I get a life sentence?" She was happy knowing what she was going to do. The painting was going to be sent to Andrea in Trapani after the show closed. She'd close the studio and go to Sicily. *I was shameless before,* she had told herself, *and I can be shameless if that's what it takes to make him understand I won't leave.* Andrea had once told her he would beg, if she wanted him to, and he was incredibly proud. *I'm not that proud.* The thought made her dizzy. *It will be easier for me to say I need him.*

Paola waved from a knot of people. She held up all ten fingers extended widely and then gestured at her mouth. They would all go and eat after the gallery closed at ten o'clock. Viviano had invited forty or fifty of his closest, dearest friends to share the celebration at Ristorante Gallo. Paola had insisted they go, saying, "It will probably be the last time the old fox ever eats with us. When the bill is presented to him, he'll depart this earth in a puff of lavender smoke."

The crowd thinned out slowly. Some stood outside in the cooler evening air, sipping wine and smoking. Viviano drifted by, his eyes on fire, and gave Torey the final report.

"Eight large acrylics, ten small ones, most of the pastels." He pressed one hand to his heart. "Two possible commissions and at least two reviews tomorrow in the papers. I swear to you on my grandchildren I would give you anything you wanted tonight!"

Torey was tempted to ask him if he could deliver a certain tall, dark Sicilian but she restrained herself. Paola was slipping back out of Viviano's office when she caught her arm, startling Paola.

"Are you hiding out tonight?" Torey whispered. "I haven't seen you for five minutes. Oh, Paola, were you smoking in there? You look very guilty!"

"Not a puff, and only two glasses of wine all night," Paola protested. "I could take Holy Orders, I've been so good lately."

"Your habit would get a bit tight in a few months." Torey laughed. "I only wanted to thank you for everything, and I mean everything. The last few days would have been impossible to get through without you or Roberto. No one has better friends," she said, putting a hand to her flushed face. "I know I'm getting sloppy and sentimental but it's not just this wine."

It seemed like a good time to exchange confidences while the evening was still glorious and magical and the last sips of wine gave Torey the courage to appear foolish. She linked her arm through Paola's as they walked through the gallery.

"I'm leaving Rome," she began.

"Oh, no, you can't!" Paola looked positively stricken. "When I said go home to Chicago, I didn't mean tonight."

"Not tonight," Torey assured her, amused at her reaction. "I made some decisions concerning Andrea. I'm sending him *Children of Sicily* as a present, perhaps to warn him, because in September I'm following the gift. I'll go there and be whatever— friend, mistress or thorn in his side—but I'm going!"

247

Paola took a deep breath. "You are really willing to risk everything, aren't you? I'd be the last one to say don't go, then." She tapped herself on the forehead with her open palm, remembering something. "What a scatterbrain I'm turning into! My brain is so full of the baby, the paintings and a meal Gaspare is paying for, I completely forgot the present! You're sending Andrea a gift, but he sent you his."

"What are you babbling about?" cried Torey. "He sent me something?"

"It's at our apartment, of course. He knew from Peppina when the show was opening and it came from Palermo. You can go and freshen up and get it, no? You look a little bit wilted. The dress is lovely, just as I said, but we can go casual to the Gallo."

"Yes, Mamma Vizzini," Torey said, delirious with the thought that Andrea had made the night perfect. "Oh, Paola, what a terrible dictator you'll be with a baby and Roberto to order around!"

"Exactly," said Paola, pushing her toward the door. "And if I'd been the lawyer in this family, we'd never lose a case. Go ahead and make it snappy. I can't wait to see what your Scarpi sent you." Paola smiled smugly to herself, watching Torey leave. She enjoyed the idea that Torey might not have to listen to endless toasts tonight.

The key to the apartment was on the ring with the car keys, and Torey fumbled for it in the dark hallway. She had trouble opening the door due to her eager anxiety. Once the clumsy, heavy lock was outwitted she slipped inside, grateful for the apartment's peace and quiet. The Vizzinis' place was so familiar she didn't bother with the light. She dropped her purse on the foyer table and headed for the living room. Her heels tapped briskly on the marble floors. Soft, golden cones of light spilled out of Roberto's study onto the old oriental rugs.

Andrea was sitting in Roberto's favorite chair, the only comfortable one in the whole apartment. A suit coat and tie were draped carelessly over the desk and a few magazines lay open on the floor.

"Andrea?" she whispered in a breathless, disbelieving voice. She tilted her head slightly to see him in the shadows. The lamp's glow caught the warm copper highlights in her hair and silvered the sheen of the rose-pink dress. "But Paola said . . ."

He stood up, all grace and elegance in motion. He started to walk toward her but stopped abruptly before he reached the doorway.

"Yes, I know what Paola said. She said what I told her to say; a package did arrive from Sicily today. I never lie, you know. Oh, Torey, I had to see you again!"

She ran to him, throwing herself into the secure warmth of his arms, unable to speak and afraid to think beyond the moment. He caught her tightly, lifting her until only her toes touched the floor. He kissed her eyelids, her throat and her mouth until she gasped for air.

"I missed you more than I can tell you," she confessed, holding her face against the front of his shirt. "I was going to wait until September and then . . ."

"September would have been too late," he said sternly. "I've been useless, no good working, no good with Benedetto since you left. I'm angry and miserable with everyone the way I was to you, Vittoria. I wanted you to stay but I couldn't ask it then." He cupped her face in his hands and let his thumbs trace the fine, high cheekbones.

Not long ago the fierce expression on his face would have frightened her because she had never seen love this clearly in his eyes. She pressed her fingers against his lips to silence him the way he had done to her on the beach at night. She kissed his cheek and let the tip of her tongue trace a familiar, sweet line to his mouth.

Andrea looked into mild, gently mocking eyes like ancient seas and was fearful of the passion in himself, an urge to crush her and devour her completely. It was a feeling he had known only with her.

"Wait, please," he whispered to her. "There's something I have to say. Do you know what I'm here to ask of you? I'm more stubborn, more proud, more difficult than even you know. I'm bound to a place and to people by ties of love and honor I can't ever break, not even for you, Torey. Vittoria, how appropriate your name is! You won a total victory over me. When I told you 'he conquers who conquers himself,' I thought I had to forget you. There was no chance you could stay with a man like me. I can't give you contentment, I'm afraid."

"I don't want that," she said softly. "We'll find a secret place for us alone, and I have a good idea where it will be." Her eyes darkened into the green of an open field. "I love Benedetto, Trapani, all the people you feel so obligated to. I love you, Andrea."

The long tremor that shook his body excited her,

and Torey felt sure he would not waste much more time in talk. He kissed her hands and thought of the ring he'd brought, an ancient gold coin with wheat on one side and Venus on the other, but he hardly dared believe she'd say what he ached to hear.

"My shining girl, you and Benedetto and I will go and give thanks soon for the gift of love from a certain lady who waits in Sicily. I promised him we'd leave Venus a gift if you said yes to me. I love you, Torey. Will you say yes? I want to make you cry with joy the way . . ." His voice deepened and broke off as he kissed her, unable to finish the sentence. When he raised his head, his blue eyes were dark with hunger for her. "If you could say yes."

She tried to say it, forming the soft hiss of *si*, but his mouth came down to capture the sound and hold it forever.

MORE ROMANCE FOR
A SPECIAL WAY TO RELAX

$1.95 each

2 ☐ Hastings	21 ☐ Hastings	41 ☐ Halston	60 ☐ Thorne
3 ☐ Dixon	22 ☐ Howard	42 ☐ Drummond	61 ☐ Beckman
4 ☐ Vitek	23 ☐ Charles	43 ☐ Shaw	62 ☐ Bright
5 ☐ Converse	24 ☐ Dixon	44 ☐ Eden	63 ☐ Wallace
6 ☐ Douglass	25 ☐ Hardy	45 ☐ Charles	64 ☐ Converse
7 ☐ Stanford	26 ☐ Scott	46 ☐ Howard	65 ☐ Cates
8 ☐ Halston	27 ☐ Wisdom	47 ☐ Stephens	66 ☐ Mikels
9 ☐ Baxter	28 ☐ Ripy	48 ☐ Ferrell	67 ☐ Shaw
10 ☐ Thiels	29 ☐ Bergen	49 ☐ Hastings	68 ☐ Sinclair
11 ☐ Thornton	30 ☐ Stephens	50 ☐ Browning	69 ☐ Dalton
12 ☐ Sinclair	31 ☐ Baxter	51 ☐ Trent	70 ☐ Clare
13 ☐ Beckman	32 ☐ Douglass	52 ☐ Sinclair	71 ☐ Skillern
14 ☐ Keene	33 ☐ Palmer	53 ☐ Thomas	72 ☐ Belmont
15 ☐ James	35 ☐ James	54 ☐ Hohl	73 ☐ Taylor
16 ☐ Carr	36 ☐ Dailey	55 ☐ Stanford	74 ☐ Wisdom
17 ☐ John	37 ☐ Stanford	56 ☐ Wallace	75 ☐ John
18 ☐ Hamilton	38 ☐ John	57 ☐ Thornton	76 ☐ Ripy
19 ☐ Shaw	39 ☐ Milan	58 ☐ Douglass	77 ☐ Bergen
20 ☐ Musgrave	40 ☐ Converse	59 ☐ Roberts	78 ☐ Gladstone

Silhouette Special Edition

MORE ROMANCE FOR
A SPECIAL WAY TO RELAX

$2.25 each

79 ☐ Hastings	85 ☐ Beckman	91 ☐ Stanford	97 ☐ Shaw
80 ☐ Douglass	86 ☐ Halston	92 ☐ Hamilton	98 ☐ Hurley
81 ☐ Thornton	87 ☐ Dixon	93 ☐ Lacey	99 ☐ Dixon
82 ☐ McKenna	88 ☐ Saxon	94 ☐ Barrie	100 ☐ Roberts
83 ☐ Major	89 ☐ Meriwether	95 ☐ Doyle	101 ☐ Bergen
84 ☐ Stephens	90 ☐ Justin	96 ☐ Baxter	102 ☐ Wallace

LOOK FOR THUNDER AT DAWN BY PATTI BECKMAN
AVAILABLE IN AUGUST AND
SUMMER COURSE IN LOVE BY CAROLE HALSTON
IN SEPTEMBER.

SILHOUETTE SPECIAL EDITION, Department SE/2
1230 Avenue of the Americas
New York, NY 10020

Please send me the books I have checked above. I am enclosing $_____
(please add 50¢ to cover postage and handling. NYS and NYC residents
please add appropriate sales tax). Send check or money order—no cash or
C.O.D.'s please. Allow six weeks for delivery.

NAME _____

ADDRESS _____

CITY _____ STATE/ZIP _____

Silhouette Special Edition

Coming Next Month

Wild Is The Heart by Abra Taylor

Tory Allworth knew the sea was Luc Devereux's lifeblood, but the same inevitability that made the waves crash against the cliffs made Tory challenge the sea for his love.

My Loving Enemy by Pat Wallace

Once Linda had been afraid to lose herself in Judd's arms. Now, however, when it seemed the tall Texan no longer wanted her, she realized Judd's arms were the only place she wanted to be.

Fair Exchange by Tracy Sinclair

Australia had never figured in Leslie's plans until she inherited an outback ranch and came into conflict with Raider MacKenzie. At first he wanted her land . . . but then he wanted her all-too-vulnerable heart.

Never Too Late by Nancy John

Grant Kilmartin had been so busy building his construction company that he had given little thought to building relationships, until he met Natalie. They clashed professionally, but personally they were in perfect harmony.

Flower Of The Orient by Erin Ross

Lisa loved everything about Japan with one exception: Keith Brannon, the man who was pitted against her beloved uncle in business. So why was he the only man she saw in her dreams?

No Other Love by Jeanne Stephens

Their lives had taken different paths—Tyler had gone to a small West Virginia town; Kristal to Houston. But miles were nothing when Kristal learned that Tyler was hurt—and when they came together for the second time, they knew it would be forever.